PLANNING THE
CHURCH
YEAR

LEONEL L. MITCHELL

PLANNING THE
CHURCH
YEAR

MOREHOUSE *MP* PUBLISHING

Morehouse Publishing

Editorial Office
871 Ethan Allen Hwy.
Suite 204
Ridgefield, CT 06877

Corporate Office
P.O. Box 1321
Harrisburg, PA 17105

Library of Congress Cataloging-in-Publication Data
Mitchell, Leonel L. (Leonel Lake), 1930-
     Planning the church year / Leonel L. Mitchell.
        p.   cm.
     Includes bibliographical references.
     ISBN 0-8192-1554-6
       1. Episcopal Church—Liturgy.   2. Anglican Communion—Liturgy.
3. Public worship—Episcopal Church.   4. Public worship—Anglican
Communion.   5. Church year.   I. Title.
BX5940.M57   1991   90-27365
264'.03—dc20   CIP

Printed in the United States of America

Second Printing, 1996

Contents

1.
What Do We Mean by Liturgical Planning?

Many Episcopalians seem to feel that, since we have a *Book of Common Prayer*, liturgical planning is unnecessary. Once upon a time, it is true, someone had to choose whether we use Rite One or Rite Two for this service. But since that has already been decided once and for all, no further planning is necessary. All you need is to get a calendar to tell you what the proper lessons are, to choose three familiar hymns from the available list of about twenty-five, to ask the choir director the name of the anthem for the program, and we are ready to start.

I hope this picture is wildly exaggerated, but I have attended many services that leave me wondering whether it is. Some parishes ignore all possible options and always conduct the service in a single inflexible way, as if this had been handed down from heaven on golden tablets. Others approach the options provided in the Prayer Book with the enthusiasm of a teenager at a "build-your-own-sundae" counter. There is no thought of congruity and coherence but boundless enthusiasm for getting some of everything.

Considering the Options

What is necessary is to consider the various options available in the services of *The Book of Common Prayer* as a part of a total program in which the individual elements are seen primarily as parts of an integrated whole, including readings, prayers, hymns, service music, and sermon. This process is called liturgical planning. If we do not plan, we soon fall short of even the minimum requirements of the Prayer Book. We sink into "We always do Rite One," or a mindless mix-and-match of incomprehensible alternatives. The individual

1

elements may be excellent, but the service itself appears to have been assembled from the menu of a Chinese restaurant, taking two items from column A, one from column B, etc. The liturgical year is neglected, and the Christmas midnight eucharist becomes distinguishable from Ash Wednesday only by the hymns and the color of the vestments. There is no continuity or integrity in the services from Sunday to Sunday, and we come to the end of a liturgical season with the feeling that there has been no overall theme or plan to what we have experienced, although some of the individual moments may have been excellent. I say these things, not from any lofty vantage point of omnicompetence from which to look down on others, but as a fellow offender and one who is twice guilty because he teaches others how to do what he so often fails to do.

Liturgy and Church Life

Liturgy is the expression of the life of the Church. It expresses our unity in the One Holy Catholic and Apostolic Church. It is our bond of unity with other Christians and in particular with those with whom we are bound *in communion*. This is not simply a technical term. It means those with whom we celebrate the eucharist and receive communion, for our common liturgy binds us together. The liturgy of *The Book of Common Prayer* identifies us as a congregation of the Episcopal Church. It visibly identifies this congregation with other congregations, and where this continuity from congregation to congregation is not apparent, we fail to manifest our unity in Christ.

The liturgy is also an expression of our congregational unity, and it is ultimately the concern of the whole people of God. The priest presides over the assembly but does not rule over the congregation. The canons of the Episcopal Church give the rector ultimate control of worship, but this can only be exercised within a congregation. A symphony conductor cannot function without a body of musicians, and a priest cannot function liturgically without a worshiping congregation.

The full, active, intelligent participation of all the people of God in the liturgy is the right and duty of every baptized man, woman, and child, by reason of their baptism, because worship is a part of the priestly activity of Jesus Christ in which the priestly people of God participate as members of the Body of which he is the Head. The eucharist, for example, is described as the sacrifice of Christ—celebrated in Head and members. Worship is not a performance by skilled professionals for a passive audience. It is the common work of a group of brothers and sisters. The Pauline churches in the New Testament clearly expected the members of the congregation to share their talents, whatever they were, in the worship of the Church.

Every congregation has its own life and tradition, including musical and liturgical traditions. Not every option in the Prayer Book and Hymnal is *really* available to every congregation. Not only are some things beyond their resources, some things "just aren't us." This is neither good nor bad but simply the way things are. Congregations, like individuals, have preferences and tastes. Golden copes and clouds of incense may or may not be a part of your tradition. One congregation prefers the guitar and "renewal" music, another sings only plainsong, while a third carefully avoids both.

Liturgical planners need to look at the life of the parish in its totality and set up general parameters for worship. They need to begin with a realistic inventory of their resources, including both people and things.

Resources for Liturgical Planning

The first resource most congregations have is a church building. It may be a blessing, a headache, an unmitigated disaster, or all three, but it exists, and discovering how best to use it is one of the planner's first tasks. Is it too small? Is crowding a problem? Or is it too large and needs to be made functionally smaller? It contains a number of fixed and movable church furnishings, such as an altar, a font, a lectern, or pulpit or both, pews or chairs, and choir stalls. These may be badly located, making it difficult for people to participate actively in the liturgy. If they are easily movable, consideration should be given to moving them, and if they are not, then planners need to consider seriously how to make the best possible use of their good features and to minimize their faults. Often people within the congregation or available for consultation in the community or through the diocese can help a congregation answer these questions.

Obviously, for worship we need a protected space where
we can gather around a table, a reading stand, and, on some
occasions, a font. Some church buildings come close to failing to meet these minimum requirements. Their setups prevent gathering, or their environments are so unfriendly as to
preclude doing anything together. Often real work is needed
to make a building built in a different time suitable for *our*
worship, but the work is worth doing.

Changing the Worship Environment

Be careful of doing things that cannot be undone, especially
if they radically alter the building. Some buildings are indeed
hideous, but most were simply built to the specifications of
an earlier age and are merely unsuited for contemporary
worship without what Pierce Middleton calls "retrofitting"
(see A. Pierce Middleton, *New Wine in Old Skins*).

The most common problem is the long chancel with an
altar at the far end that produces a tunnel effect, especially if
the choir stalls are empty. One of the most simple and
straightforward solutions, if the chancel is nice looking, is to
build a new altar at the crossing, thereby moving the action
down to the level of the people. The choir can continue to
occupy the choir pews, and seats for clergy and acolytes can
be moved out toward the center. The chancel itself can then
be used as a chapel for small services, with people sitting in
the choir stalls.

Often, changing communities leave congregations with
churches much too large. Using banners and screens to create new and smaller space often works, as does roping off
back pews—or removing them. An open space might be created around the font, for example, where the baptismal parties could stand with the congregation at baptisms.
Whatever the problem, imagination is the first step to a solu-
tion.

The Prayer Book and Hymnal as Resources

The Book of Common Prayer and *The Hymnal 1982* are
perhaps obvious resources for liturgical planning, but they
are often overlooked. The Prayer Book not only contains the
texts of prayers and directions for the conduct of the ser-

vices but is a guide for the use of other resources. The Hymnal, in addition to the music, contains indexed lists of hymns, metrical psalms and canticles, hymns based on specific liturgical texts, hymns for children, and a liturgical index. A copier will make it possible to reproduce materials, such as those included in the appendix of *The Hymnal 1982* or in *Gradual Psalms*, for congregational use as well as service bulletins.

People as Resources

It is important to identify the people available to fill specific roles in the liturgy: readers, acolytes, lay eucharistic ministers, oblation bearers, singers, dancers, instrumental musicians (organ and guitar are not the only possibilities), and ordained clergy (priests and deacons). People are also needed to prepare for the celebration: altar guild members, bread bakers, wine makers, bulletin preparers (typists and/or calligraphers), and artists. Another list includes those whose skills will be needed if the congregation decides to make alterations in their environment for worship: architects, carpenters, decorators, artists, and people with visual imagination.

Make the inventory first. Discover what is possible before you decide what you want to do. Then decide what you as a congregation are trying to do in worship. If you could do what you (the rector and a representative group of parishioners) think would be best, what would it look like? It may be helpful to let your fantasy take over and be creative. Then look at your inventory of resources and see which things you have the resources to do. Perhaps you can't do exactly what you would like, but you *do* have the resources to do *something*.

Start by thinking of the liturgy itself. How do you involve the congregation actively and intelligently in the worship of God on Sunday morning? The answer is not some kind of gimmick. It is careful planning *with* members of the congregation. One way to enhance participation is simply to involve people in the planning of the particular service and in its celebration.

The Liturgical Year

The liturgical year and its accompanying lectionary is, of course, a major resource for planning. The lectionary was compiled with a clear purpose in view: to proclaim the Paschal mystery of the death and resurrection of Jesus Christ and our participation in those mighty events. In making this choice, the lectionary committee was faithful to the underlying nature of the liturgical year. Neither the lectionary nor the liturgical year is a lesson plan for teaching systematic theology, Bible stories, or even the "history of salvation." The purpose is to proclaim and draw us into the saving events of the death, resurrection, and ascension of Jesus Christ and our participation in them through faith and in baptism, so that the victory that has been won in Christ is being won by him in us.

Marianne Micks, in *The Future Present*, distinguishes between what she calls a "tourist view" of the Church Year, which takes us on a guided walk through the Holy Land with Jesus, and the mysteriological, or traditional, view that in a real sense we participate in the events we celebrate. "*This* is the night," we proclaim in the Easter Vigil, "when all who believe in Christ are delivered from the gloom of sin, and are restored to grace and holiness of life. This is the night when Christ broke the bonds of death and hell, and rose victorious from the grave." It is more than a convenient occasion to preach about the resurrection, "This is the night!"

Sunday as the Lord's Day; Lent, Holy Week, and Easter as the core of the liturgical year; proclamation of the good news that God in Christ "has visited and redeemed his people" as the primary content of our preaching—these are the core of this celebration. They are what constitute the liturgical year as it has been celebrated in the Church from the patristic age.

If we are going to plan the year in accordance with its own principles of development, we need to think of it as falling into two cycles. The first is the Lent-Easter-Pentecost cycle. This has as its core the celebration of the Great Vigil and our Lord's "passover" from death to life. The central theme, not only of the Vigil but of the Christian year, is our passage with Christ through the grave to the risen life, celebrated in baptism, in eucharist, and in the Easter festival. The theme is extended throughout the eight days of Holy Week, beginning with the passion narrative on Palm Sunday and especially in the liturgies of Maundy Thursday and Good Friday. The Great Fifty Days, the period from Easter to Pentecost, with its first readings from Acts and its Gospel readings from the Fourth Gospel, give us the opportunity to celebrate the resurrection begun in Christ, continued in the life of the apostolic church, and working still in us. It encompasses Ascension Day and the Day of Pentecost, which are parts of the whole seasonal celebration. Finally, all of this is introduced by the Lenten fast. Here the Sunday Gospels give us the themes.

The second cycle is Advent-Christmas-Epiphany. This is not a different celebration from the older Easter cycle but a different look at the same mystery. The twelve-day Christmas-Epiphany celebration of the Incarnation and manifestation of Christ ("The Word became flesh and dwelt among us; and we have beheld the glory") leads into the Baptism of Our Lord and our participation in his divine life. The Christ who died and rose again for us took flesh of the Virgin "for us and for our salvation." From the Second Sunday in Advent through the Baptism of Our Lord, this is our theme. The nativity, the adoration of the Magi, the baptism are all ways of looking into our union with the Incarnate One.

The rest of the year, called by the original Roman Catholic compilers of the lectionary "ordinary time," is considered by Episcopalians as two quasi-seasons: the Sundays after Epiphany and the Sundays after Pentecost. I call them quasi-seasons because they are not real seasons. The weekly celebration of the resurrection on the Lord's Day is their primary focus.

The Sundays after Epiphany are the better organized. They are framed by the Baptism of Our Lord at the beginning and the transfiguration Gospel on the last Sunday. This makes it possible to look at the Sundays as a series of "manifestations." The much longer season after Pentecost has no organization. Trinity Sunday at its beginning and Christ the King at its end provide a sort of loose frame. Toward its end, the post-Pentecost season develops a real structure. Its theme is the Second Coming, and it finds its climax in the First Sunday of Advent of the following year. Advent 1, like all new year's festivals, looks both forward and back. It completes the Pentecost-to-Advent transition and turns from the Second Advent to the First, modulating back into preparation for Christmas.

This is the heart of liturgical celebration, and if we begin our planning here and not with, "Can we sing my favorite hymn?" or "Shall we use incense this week?" we shall be proclaiming and celebrating the Gospel and not simply reading it. This, of course, means that celebrations need to be planned for the year, rather than one service at a time.

2.
Who Should Do
the Liturgical Planning?

Rectors or Vicars are canonically responsible for the worship of the congregation. The canons also direct that they seek the assistance of "persons skilled in music" and "together" see that music appropriate to its liturgical context is used. There is no requirement that they consult with anyone else.

The Parish Priest as Planner

In many ways the ordained priest seems an ideal choice for parish liturgical planner. He or she has almost certainly studied liturgics in the course of preparation for the ministry and will have information and insights that other worshipers lack. The priest will be the usual presider and preacher at the parish liturgies and is, therefore, in a position both to understand and to implement the necessary planning. If the priest takes this responsibility seriously, then the services should be well and coherently planned. In many congregations, the rector or vicar has traditionally assumed this responsibility and has produced services that are both beautiful and worshipful. In small congregations, the parish musician is often a part-time accompanist with no expertise in liturgical music, and the priest becomes the sole planner by default.

The parish priest as sole planner, however, has the weaknesses as well as the strengths of an individual operation. What is gained in singleness of outlook is often lost in narrowness of vision, and the beautiful services fail to meet the needs of the congregation. In parishes where there is more than one priest, the participation of the priests who will preside at particular services seems almost essential. In the same way, a parish deacon should be a part of the planning process. The deacon not only has a significant role in the celebration of the liturgy but is specifically charged "to interpret to the Church the needs, concerns, and hopes of the world" (*Book of Common Prayer*, hereafter *BCP*, p. 543). This concern, applied to liturgical planning, should help to rescue services from irrelevance by bringing vital and different concerns to the planning process.

Staff Planning

In large parishes, the planning is often done by the professional staff: clergy, musicians, and perhaps a director of Christian education. I have taken part in such a weekly staff liturgical planning meeting in a cathedral congregation. The bishop, five priests, two deacons, the organist, and a lay assistant provided an interesting and competent mix with a good deal of expertise. There was a wealth of good ideas, a fair amount of give and take, and good liturgy. The obvious lack was congregational representation. Our concerns were admittedly clerical. The Roman sacramentary says,

> In planning the celebration, the priest should consider the spiritual good of the assembly rather than his own desires. The choice of texts is to be made in consultation with the ministers and others who have a function in the celebration *including the faithful* . . . [i.e., the members of the congregation]. (General Instruction of the Roman Missal, par. 313)

This is excellent advice. Lay people generally have a better feel than clergy do for their own congregation. It is better to argue about the competing claims of Pentecost and Mothers' Day when planning the service than to have to discuss it with angry parishioners after the celebration.

The Parish Worship Committee

A parish worship (or liturgy) committee (including clergy, parish musicians, lay readers, and congregational representatives) is the ideal group for making the general decisions we have been discussing, looking at the life of the parish in its totality, and setting up general parameters for worship. These committee members can consider not only the congregation's resources but its expectations for its liturgy. They are better equipped than any individual or professional staff, no matter how competent, to decide what the characteristics of the parish's worship will be.

These characteristics include important but seldom discussed questions such as the following:
• How formal or informal should the style of our parish liturgy be? There is no right answer to this question, but that does not mean that members of the congregation, including ordained members, do not have strongly held views on the subject.
• What kind of music do we want? Healey Willan and three familiar hymns? A wide variety of hymns and service music from *The Hymnal 1982*? Songs of celebration, either from the booklet of that title or some other appendix to the official hymnal? Then we need to ask whether all the music should be sung by the congregation or whether some pieces are the offering of the choir. We can then go on to ask how large a place music should have in our services. Again, there is no correct answer except in terms of the specific congregation. The Hymnal provides musical settings for almost the entire service. This does not mean every congregation will or should sing everything. The canons require that music be used "as an offering to the glory of God and as a help to the people in their worship. . . ." What music and how much music are questions to be decided locally.
• What is the style of our parish liturgy? This is a question often left to the rector or vicar to decide, not always happily for the congregation. When it is discussed, it is often by a vestry criticizing the parish priest or by a search committee seeking a new one. Even then the answer is frequently a single stereotypical word: *low, catholic, charismatic, renewed, central*. A description of what the congregation expects to happen on Sundays with some clear idea of how much variety is acceptable is more helpful.
• How much change will there be in the liturgy from Sunday to Sunday? Many congregations will wish to find a liturgical format and keep it almost untouched. Others will wish to change not only texts but manner of performance from week to week, singing the psalms, for example, to simplified Anglican chants sometimes, reading them responsively at others, and using the settings in *Gradual Psalms* on still other occasions. Sometimes such

changes can be effectively used to mark the changes in liturgical seasons.
• What use should be made of Rite One and Rite Two? The answer does not have to be engraved in stone, and it is a good idea to raise the question again every year or two.

One of the common features of all of these questions is that they are best answered by representative groups of parishioners. Not only will the answers be more likely to represent the actual feelings of the congregation, but it becomes possible to involve the liturgy committee in creative liturgical change. If the committee is convinced that changes need to be made, it becomes the committee's function, not just the priest's, to promote the changes in the congregation. The more people involved in the planning, the more people have a vested interest in its going well. Of course, if it goes badly, the committee, not the vicar or rector, takes the blame, and it is possible to step back without causing a rift between priest and people, for the decisions have been joint decisions.

Role of the Clergy

Some rectors feel comfortable allowing a layperson to chair the parish worship committee and serving themselves as a member and resource. Others choose to chair the committee themselves. In either case, it is important that the clergy be members of the committee, so that their informed voices will be a part of the discussion. For the rector or vicar to take no part in the discussion and simply veto the decisions of the liturgy committee is counterproductive.

Sometimes clergy, faced for the first time with a prospect of a parish liturgy committee doing liturgical planning, have an identity crisis and begin to wonder exactly what the ministry of the priest *is* in this process. First and foremost the priest is an enabler, one who makes it possible for the people to worship. My analogy is the conductor of an orchestra. The conductor usually does not play the music personally, but he or she enables the orchestra to work together to do it. This means that the priest has a designated role as presider. The priest is a *minister* of the liturgy, not its master. He or she *serves* the Body of Christ to enable the priestly people of God to fulfill their baptismal priesthood. Priests also have personal talents not conferred by ordination but either innate or acquired. By education and training they are preachers, exegetes of Scripture, and liturgical resources. They may be singers and possess other useful and usable skills. They must be willing to use the talents of others and not usurp their roles in the worship.

If there is a parish deacon, it is the *deacon's* responsibility to supervise and train lay people for their ministries, in the liturgy and in the world. But neither priest nor deacon are to do the job for them. The best model I can hold up for the Church is the Boy and Girl Scouts. They have professional leadership, but most of the grass-roots work is done by volunteers whom the professionals train.

Everything needs to be brought to the altar at the parish eucharist, and from the altar, the power of God goes forth into all these activities of Christians in the Church and in the world. All we really need to do the liturgy of the Church is a priest to preside, a leader of song, and a community that wants to worship. Yet the whole parish can be involved in the planning and the doing of it.

Clergy should not be afraid to use their own skills or to make way for others to use theirs. Ordained ministers are not diminished by someone who does things better than they do, unless they try to prevent them from doing it.

The committee should be set up initially by the parish priest, who should appoint the first members. The committee can then decide to increase its own membership by adding those it comes to see that it needs. Its scope of authority should also be spelled out clearly at the beginning. It can be an advisory committee to the rector or vicar, presenting its conclusions to the priest for canonical approval, or it can be a decision-making body to which the priest delegates the planning responsibility. It is important that the committee understand which it is.

In addition to this sort of overall planning for worship, the liturgy committee needs to look each year at the liturgical year and other parish calendars (when church school starts, public school vacations, etc.) and decide the shape of the entire year's worship. They need to decide what the congregation will do *this year* to mark off Advent, Lent, and Easter, the major liturgical seasons, and what will be done to distinguish festivals from ordinary Sundays. They need to integrate into the liturgical calendar local parish celebrations (and anticipate problems that might interfere with church attendance on particular days). The point is that unless these things are decided for the whole year, or at least for a liturgical season, there will be perceived discontinuity from Sunday to Sunday.

To plan a specific service, the celebrant, preacher, and music director would be the minimum planning group. To this minimum it helps to add the deacon (if there is one), readers, leader of the Prayers of the People, an usher, and representative singers and congregation members. Sometimes parish liturgy committees find it convenient to divide into subcommittees, which may involve additional people not members of the main committee, to plan the individual services, each subcommittee serving for a liturgical season.

Often planning can be well done by ad hoc planning groups. Ideally, these are created by the parish worship committee. They are effective means of planning special services, such as the Easter Vigil, the bishop's visitation, or a service commemorating those with AIDS. People with special interests who are unwilling or unable to serve on the parish committee will be active members of these ad hoc groups.

3.
Getting Started on Planning

Once the parish liturgy committee has dealt with the major issues of environment, style, rite, and seasonal variations, it becomes the task of that committee, or some subcommittee, to plan for individual services. In the following chapters, we shall consider the requirements of the different liturgical seasons, but we shall begin by planning a generic Sunday eucharist, since this is material that we shall need to use for planning almost all services.

Start with the Readings

Begin by asking if there is a specific given "theme" for the day. On Christmas or Palm Sunday the answer is obviously yes, but on many Sundays there is no clear theme, and one should not be manufactured. If there is one, however, it needs to be stated by the planners and consciously used. Then look at the liturgical readings. If there are options among them, decide which will actually be read. Three lessons are normatively used on Sundays and two on weekdays that are not major holy days. They need to be clearly and intelligibly read by lay people. The lectors should be selected as soon as possible, and, if they are not already members of the planning group, it is helpful if they become part of it for the service at which they will read. The Gospel is read (or sung) by the deacon, if there is one. If there is no deacon, an assisting priest or the celebrant reads the Gospel. It may be read from the lectern, the pulpit, or the center aisle. The procession to the place where it is read may include processional torches, and incense may be carried before the Gospel book, which symbolizes the presence of Christ, the living Word.

Options for the Psalm

Consider the options for the psalm and how it will be done. The Prayer Book suggests several traditional methods of psalmody (*BCP*, 582ff). Any of these methods may be used either to recite or sing the psalms. The psalms are, of course, ancient hymns and were intended to be sung. Congregational psalm singing has a distinguished history in Jewish and Christian worship, and churches of many denominations are rediscovering the joy of singing the psalms. Lutherans, Presbyterians, Methodists, and Roman Catholics, for example, have included music and suggestions for singing the psalms in their new service books or hymnals, all intended to enable the congregation to join in these biblical hymns. Reciting hymns, no matter how beautiful the words, is, after all, not the same as singing them.

Three ways of singing the psalms are readily available to the average congregation. The appendix to the Hymnal contains a number of simplified Anglican chants (S 408–S 416) that can be used to sing the psalm either by the entire congregation in unison or antiphonally between the sides of the congregation, the congregation and choir, or men and women. This method can be effectively used even by quite small congregations. The use of the same simple chant every week with the appointed psalm portions tends to overcome people's feeling of not knowing the tune, and many small rural congregations without professional musicians are regularly singing the psalm at the Sunday liturgy.

Church Hymnal Corporation publishes *Gradual Psalms*, containing simple plainsong settings to the eucharistic psalms with refrains. Permission is given to reproduce either the refrain or the entire psalm for congregational use. In this method, the psalm verses are sung either by a cantor or by the choir with the congregation joining in the refrain. It is one of the most ancient and the simplest methods of psalm singing, since the congregation sings only a single repeated refrain.

The third method is to sing metrical psalms. This tradition, which comes from the Reformed Church of Geneva, has a long and honorable history in Anglicanism. There are many metrical psalms, and hymns based on psalms in the Hymnal. A numerical index of these is in the appendix on page 679.

There are also many collections of metrical psalms, including *A New Metrical Psalter* (Church Hymnal Corp.) arranged for singing the psalms appointed in the lectionary to be used between the lessons. Even if the congregation has never sung the psalms, it is worth trying, at least occasionally. Certainly every congregation can sing a metrical psalm to a familiar tune.

Sermon Theme

Next ask the preacher for the theme of the sermon. It should flow out of the readings, and the other choices need to be related to it.

Beginning the Service

Now you are ready to go back to the beginning of the service. A number of decisions will have already been made as a part of your overall planning. Usually the Rite One/Rite Two decision will have been made, but if not, it should be made next. Whether or not to begin with the Penitential Order should also be decided now, not on a service-by-service basis. Some places may wish never so to begin, while others will always wish to do so. At the very least, this decision should be made for a liturgical season. Beginning with the Penitential Order sets a penitential tone for the service. It is hard to move from it to the *Gloria* or another festal hymn. This might be an option to use during Lent. On the other hand, some people feel that, by using the penitential material at the beginning, it can be treated as a preparation for a festal service without further penitential elements.

The Prayer Book provides for the service to begin with a hymn, psalm, or anthem. The anthem might well be a canticle. Most of the time you will choose to begin with an entrance hymn. Beginning with a chant has a different feeling than beginning with a hymn and one worth using for particular occasions. Another possibility is to enter to organ music or in silence and begin with the acclamation. This works well if you are going to sing Gloria in excelsis or a hymn of praise, and it avoids putting two major vocal pieces so close together at the beginning.

Gloria, Kyrie, or What?

Shall we sing the *Gloria in excelsis*, *Kyrie eleison*, *Trisagion*, or a hymn of praise? The Prayer Book directs that the Gloria, or "some other song of praise," be used from Christmas through Epiphany and on the Sundays of Eastertide and be omitted during Advent and Lent. But it makes no other recommendations. Again, setting a policy is better than making separate decisions for individual services. Sometimes only *Gloria* will do (e.g., Christmas and, perhaps, Easter). Kyrie eleison ("Lord, have mercy") has been the traditional choice for ordinary occasions. *Trisagion* ("Holy God, Holy and Mighty") is an ancient hymn of praise used at the beginning of the Byzantine liturgy. It is less obviously festive than *Gloria in excelsis* and works well both during Lent and for ordinary Sundays. The Supplement to Volume I of the Accompaniment Edition of The Hymnal 1982 (S 355) suggests canticles that might possibly be used at this place. A metrical hymn either here or at the opening can set a particular tone for the service and the possibility should not be overlooked. The hymn "Christ, the Fair Glory of the Holy Angels" (hymn 282/283), for example, makes an excellent choice as a replacement for *Gloria in excelsis* on the feast of St. Michael and All Angels.

Sermon Hymns

Any necessary decisions about the readings, or (on a few occasions) choices between alternative collects, will have been already made, and the sermon topic already settled. A hymn between the Gospel and the sermon is not an option envisioned by the Prayer Book, as it interrupts the natural connection between the readings and the exposition of the Word. A hymn after the sermon does not do violence to the structure, but it does obscure the creed as a response to the Word and also tends to put the thought of the sermon out of the congregation's mind—a mixed blessing.

The creed is an option on weekdays, but most planning will be for Sunday or major holy day services, so it will be either said or sung.

Prayers of the People

The Prayers of the People provide a bevy of options. Which form to use can be decided thematically by service or by season. The forms in the Prayer Book are intended to be suggestions, and choice is not limited to them as long as the required objects are prayed for. How the prayers are to be done requires more thought than is usually given to it. *The Book of Common Prayer* never contemplates the celebrant leading the prayers. As Prayers of the People, they are appropriately led by a member of the congregation in street clothes or by the deacon, if one is present. They may be said or sung. They are Prayers of the People, and the people must be given an opportunity to pray. Birthday blessings, prayers for anniversaries, etc., should be integrated into them.

The Prayer Book permits omitting "on occasion" the confession of sin. A congregation may choose never to do so. But if it is to be omitted sometimes, a decision must be made as to when.

The Offertory

The offertory is an action—bringing the bread and wine and money to the altar and setting the table. It will normally always be done the same way. But it needs to be planned to be sure that lay people and, if there are any, deacons take their proper part and that their role is clear. Normally this involves lay people bringing the elements, the alms, and anything else to be offered from the congregation to the altar, where they are received by a deacon or assisting priest. Only if there is no other ordained minister present are they brought to the celebrant. There is no reason why the lay people should not bring the elements directly to the altar, without the intervention of acolytes. Having acolytes intercept the alms and oblation bearers at the altar rail tends to perpetuate the myth that only clergy and people dressed to look like clergy may enter the sanctuary. Music during the offertory is a part of the offering and may represent the offering of the choir, or the congregation may sing a hymn or psalm.

Which Eucharistic Prayer?

The Great Thanksgiving, or eucharistic prayer, is the central prayer of the service, and the choice of one among the alternatives is a significant element in the planning. The presiding priest should certainly be a contributor to the decision. In Rite One, Eucharistic Prayer I is good for Lent, while II is better for ordinary use, since it includes a thanksgiving for creation. On the other hand, if the congregation has a particular attachment to Prayer I, it might be used whenever Rite One was celebrated. In Rite Two, Eucharistic Prayer A is a good choice for ordinary Sundays. Prayer B is appropriate for Advent through the Baptism of Our Lord, because of its incarnational emphasis. Prayer C is quite penitential in content and is a good alternative Lenten choice to A. It is always good for small groups where you wish to encourage participation and for informal occasions. Prayer D is long but tells the biblical story. It is ecumenical and ancient. It is a good choice for Maundy Thursday and major occasions when you do not feel the need to use the proper preface, since proper prefaces are used only with Prayers A and B. Prayer D is the only one that includes intercessions and is, therefore, useful when it is desirable to leave out the Prayers of the People, as at a baptism. Prayers B and D provide the possibility of including a saint's name and are, therefore, good choices for saint's days.

The version of the Lord's Prayer, and the decision to say or sing it, should be a part of overall planning.

Fraction Anthem

The fraction anthem is sung during the breaking of the bread. "Christ our Passover is sacrificed for us" is the most commonly used anthem, but *The Book of Occasional Services* and the Hymnal contain many alternatives. If you must break up real bread and fill a number of cups, a fraction anthem long enough to cover the action is a real option. The action goes on during the anthem. If the service is without music, either "Christ our Passover" or *Agnus Dei* is the best choice.

After Communion

A hymn may be sung *before* the postcommunion prayer. This is not a communion hymn but a new hymn to start the postcommunion section of the service. If this option is taken, it will probably be the final hymn of the service.

Rite Two contains two alternative postcommunion prayers. They can be used in some rational manner, perhaps changing them with the season.

Although one is frequently sung, the Prayer Book does not contemplate a recessional hymn. A hymn may be sung after the postcommunion prayer and the (blessing and) dismissal given from the back of the church, or a hymn may be sung here and the exit be to instrumental music.

In Rite Two, the blessing is optional. It may be omitted entirely, or one of the seasonal alternatives in *The Book of Occasional Services* may be used. Their use may form a part of seasonal planning. The dismissal follows the blessing. It is intended to be the final words of the service, after which the people leave. Historically, "Let us bless the Lord" was intended for occasions when the congregation was not, in fact, leaving.

All of these decisions must be made for every service, either by a planning group or by someone else. If there is to be consistency from Sunday to Sunday, this planning must be integrated into the overall liturgical planning for the year, to which we now turn.

4.
Planning for Advent

One of the major problems of any calendar is knowing when the new year begins. Most calendars we see begin on January 1. In Sunday school we learned that Advent Sunday was the beginning of the liturgical year. For many business people, the fiscal year begins on July 1. In most parishes, in spite of what the church calendar says, the "new year" begins when people come back from vacation, the Christian education program starts up again, and the summer schedule gives way to the regular round of parish activities.

In many senses, we already made use of this year for planning. Our organizations and educational programs generally plan their activities from September to June, and there is much to be said for looking at the fall as a time to plan the worship activities for the coming year. A number of basic decisions can be made for the entire year beginning in the fall. These include decisions about music, the role of the various choirs, the participation of children in the Sunday liturgy, arranging baptism and confirmation dates and the programs of preparation for them. If a congregation is contemplating making changes in the format or style of its services, often planning for the "school year" has much to be said for it.

The Climax of the Church Year

The First Sunday of Advent is not only the beginning of a new season, it is really the climax and conclusion of the Church Year. The apocalyptic readings leading up to the Christ the King propers on the Last Sunday after Pentecost reach their climax in the celebration of the Parousia on Advent Sunday, after which the theme rapidly modulates to the first Advent. Planning needs to take account of this continuity, so that eschatological themes are not suddenly introduced on a single Sunday and then trundled quickly off again. These eschatological readings give to the liturgy of the last few Sundays before Advent an aura of intense expectation, which should be reflected in other aspects of the liturgy.

A reasonable procedure for overall planning would be to plan the month of November, from All Saints' Day to Christ the King, with the building Advent theme, as a unit. The use of the lectionary in planning, the setting of seasonal themes for decoration of the church (such as late fall flowers), a uniform treatment of the psalm between the readings (singing or reciting it responsorially as described on p. 582 of the Prayer Book, for example), and the use of an appropriate canticle such as 9 ("The First Song of Isaiah") or 19 ("The Song of the Redeemed") throughout the period in place of the *Gloria in excelsis* are possible ways to draw the period together. Thanksgiving Day will occur on the Fourth Thursday of the month and can easily be included in the planning.

Advent as a Season

Advent itself should be planned as a distinct liturgical season. It is the season of preparation for the coming of Jesus Christ, both his coming in history to Bethlehem at Christmas and his coming in glory at the end of time "to judge the living and the dead" to which Christians look forward. Expectation, not penitence, is its major theme. "The King shall come!" and "Rejoice!" are its watchwords. The great Advent figures who dominate the scripture readings are Isaiah, John the Baptist, and the Virgin Mary.

Liturgical Color

Royal purple or Sarum blue, as colors more appropriate to the season, are increasingly used for vestments and hangings in place of the violet introduced in the nineteenth century from the Roman sequence of liturgical colors but which many people feel tended to make the season more penitential. In some places, rose vestments have been worn on the Third Sunday of Advent, also following a Roman tradition. This Sunday was known as *Gaudete* Sunday by Roman Catholics and Lutherans, because the antiphon on its introit psalm was "Rejoice in the Lord always," from the Epistle to the Philippians (4:4). If the parish owns and wishes to use such vestments, they might be more appropriate on the Fourth Sunday, where the propers are always festive and the Virgin Mary (often represented as a mystic rose) is central to the Gospel lesson. There does not seem to be any good reason to introduce rose vestments where they have not been used.

Sunday Liturgies

The Sunday morning Advent liturgies should have a seasonal unity. The Gloria is not used, and either the *Trisagion* or the *Kyrie* is sung. The use of the same setting of one of these for the four Sundays will begin to give the services continuity. The *Benedictus* is the traditional Advent canticle, and, unless it is being sung at Morning Prayer, the planners may wish to make a place for it at the eucharist. It could be sung, for example, as an entrance song or between the New Testament reading and the Gospel, either to a plainsong or Anglican chant setting from the Hymnal, depending on the preference of the congregation.

Sermons for the four Sundays can be planned as a unity, not necessarily a series, covering the major themes of the season as highlighted in the readings for the particular Sunday. If the same person will not preach every week, it is especially important that the planning committee give attention to the total impact of the Advent preaching. The sermon themes and the readings will then form the basis for selecting hymns and anthems. At least this much of the planning will have to be done well in advance, so that the music can be selected and rehearsed.

Unless different forms of the prayers of the People tied to the readings (such as those in Gail Ramshaw's *Intercessions for the Christian People*) are used every week, a decision can be made to use the same form for the whole of Advent, further tying the services together. The Advent proper preface is used at all services, and Eucharistic Prayer B, with its strong emphasis on the Incarnation, is a particularly appropriate choice for the period from Advent 1 through the Baptism of Christ.

The singing of one of the alternative fraction anthems

(*confractoria*), such as "My flesh is food indeed" (S 168 or S 169), in place of "Christ our Passover" during the breaking of the bread is another way to give seasonal unity to the services.

Two alternative seasonal blessings for Advent are in *The Book of Occasional Services* (p. 20f). The first contains four short paragraphs, to which all respond "Amen." The second is a simple introduction to the usual blessing. Either may be used, and a decision to use one or the other at every service during Advent is another seasonal possibility.

The Advent Wreath

The lighting of an Advent wreath is an appropriate seasonal symbol. The wreath is of evergreen with four candles, which may be white or the color of the Advent vestments. One candle is lighted for each of the four weeks of Advent. This is done at the beginning of the liturgy and may also be done by people in their homes. Often a fifth candle in the middle of the wreath, the Christ candle, is lighted on Christmas and throughout the twelve days. In the church, the wreath may be hung from the ceiling or placed on a stand or table in any convenient place where it can be seen by the people. *The Book of Occasional Services* (p. 28) recommends that no particular ceremonial elaboration accompany its use but that at morning services it simply be lighted before the services begin. For services held in the evening, the candles may be lighted after the Prayer for Light in the Order for Evening.

Evening Services

The use of the Order for Evening during Advent is particularly appropriate, since sunset will be early, evenings long, and evening services easily begun in a darkened church. The order may replace the entrance rite of the eucharist or be a separate evening service.

The order begins with a special greeting, "Light and peace, in Jesus Christ our Lord," and continues with a Prayer for Light. During Advent this is the collect for Advent 1. The appropriate number of candles on the Advent wreath are then lighted and the lights in the church brought up. A proper Advent *Lucernarium* (Anthem at the Candle Lighting) is given on page 10 of *The Book of Occasional Services*

and set to music in the Hymnal appendix (S 309). This may
be sung by a cantor or other song leader while the candles
are being lighted, or this may be done in silence. Then either
the hymn *Phos Hilaron* (as in Evening Prayer) "or some
other hymn" is sung. Advent has a particularly suitable hymn
for this purpose. "Creator of the stars at night" (hymn 60). If
the service is a eucharist, it continues with the collect of the
day. Otherwise it continues with an evening psalm; a lesson;
a sermon, if desired; the *Magnificat* or another canticle or
hymn of praise; prayers; and a blessing. One of the forms for
the eucharistic prayers of the people or Suffrages B from
Evening Prayer, concluding with the collect of the day and
the Lord's Prayer, are good choices for the prayers. The blessing may be the proper seasonal blessing from *The Book of
Occasional Services.*

One or more evening services, whether the eucharist or
evensong, might be considered as special events for the Advent season. *The Book of Occasional Services* contains instructions for an Advent Festival of Lessons and Music,
which is another possibility for an evening service introduced by the lighting of the Advent wreath. This will provide an opportunity for the singing of more traditional
Advent music than is convenient in four Sunday services and
give the choir an opportunity to sing some things too difficult for congregational singing, as well as serving as a parish
pre-Christmas party.

Advent Music

There is a wealth of Advent hymnody and anthems. In selecting appropriate music, remember that the Parousia theme of
Advent 1 has been replaced by the Annunciation or Visitation by Advent 4. The hymns about coming in glory are,
therefore, best for the last Sundays after Pentecost and Advent Sunday, so that by the Sunday before Christmas we can
use hymns like *Rosa Mystica* (hymn 81) or annunciation/vis-
itation hymns.

Decorating the Church

A perennial cause of conflict between "purists" and "pragmatists" is the proper time to decorate the church for Christmas. In reaction to the secular putting up of Christmas

decorations in October, purists insist that nothing can be done until December 24, while the pragmatists plead that such a course of action is totally impractical and urge an earlier date. There is, of course, no reason why evergreens and wreaths cannot be used to decorate the church during Advent. Some churches put bows of Advent blue or purple (depending upon which color they use for the altar hangings and vestments) on their wreaths, changing them to red or white for Christmas. An alternative tradition is to "green" the church on December 17, so that the greens are in place for the festive liturgies of Advent 4. This may have the "practical" advantage of keeping the greens from drying out before Epiphany. December 17 is called "O Sapientia" because a special antiphon was sung before and after the *Magnificat* at evensong from that date until Christmas. These antiphons are preserved in the Hymnal (with the dates on which they were sung) as the verses of "O come, O come, Emmanuel," (hymn 56). The "greening" of the church and the use of this special music marked the increased sense of expectation as Christmas approached. A liturgy committee with imagination might find interesting ways to adapt and incorporate these medieval customs into their own preparation for Christmas.

Start Planning Early

All of this planning needs to be at least begun by Labor Day. Your first fall planning meeting should be able to revise and complete early plans for Advent and begin planning for Christmas. Music requires preparation time, changes in schedule need to be announced well in advance, and decorations often require more than a few days to get ready.

Perhaps all of this planning seems excessive. It is not. The liturgy appears to be the most spontaneous and natural when it is the fruit of disciplined preparation and can be entered into with joy and abandon, without having to worry about what happens next. Good liturgy does not need to be complicated. Simple liturgy can be most effective, but sloppy or ill-planned worship will be satisfying to no one.

5.
Planning for the Twelve Days of Christmas

Theoretically, no season should present fewer difficulties for planning than Christmas. It is a principal feast, usually with one of the largest congregations of the year. It has some of the best and best-known music, a clear theme, immense popularity, and people expect everything at the Christmas services to be done to the best of everyone's ability. In practice, there are many problems. Christmas is a victim of its secular success. Christmas carols have been playing in shopping malls for months. Everyone is so busy getting ready for Christmas that it is hard to find time for liturgical planning, choir and acolyte rehearsals, or altar work. Often children are so excited about the coming of Santa Claus that it is difficult to get their attention to celebrate the coming of Christ.

Christmas celebrates the birth of our Lord and the Incarnation of the Divine Word. Its principal Gospel reading is John 1:1–14, not the Lukan account of the birth in Bethlehem (Luke 2:1–14) traditionally read at the first eucharistic celebration (the "midnight mass"). *The Book of Common Prayer* gives three different sets of readings for the day, as well as readings for Evening Prayer on Christmas Eve and both Morning and Evening Prayer on Christmas Day. Few congregations will have occasion to use all of them.

A Service Involving Children

The scheduling of Christmas services should be one of the first concerns of the liturgy committee. A nighttime, although not necessarily midnight, eucharist has become the principal Christmas service in most congregations. At least one service should be scheduled for Christmas Day. It is important that thought be given to including the children of the parish in the Christmas celebration, and many congregations plan an early evening service on Christmas Eve, often beginning with a procession to the crèche, especially for younger children and their families. They often find older parishioners also like to come at an earlier hour.

Either the first or second set of readings, including the Lukan nativity Gospel, is usually the best choice for this service. Familiar Christmas carols and hymns can be sung and the most familiar service music used. If there is a junior choir, they might well lead the singing. *The Book of Occasional Services* (p. 34f) contains prayers to be used at a station (or stop) at the crèche during the entrance procession. Children can bring the figures (or at least the figure of the Christ Child) to the crèche at this time and the nativity scene be set in place.

There are really no good alternatives to *Gloria in excelsis* for Christmas, but if it is not feasible to sing it at this service, it is better to sing a hymn such as "Angels we have heard on high" (hymn 96), with its refrain of "Gloria in excelsis Deo," than to recite the *Gloria*. People usually sing on festive occasions, and to recite the song the angels sang really seems to reduce the element of festivity.

The first of the three Prayer Book collect works best for a Christmas Eve service. Eucharistic Prayer B, or Eucharistic Prayer II in Rite One, are appropriate choices. One of the fraction anthems including "Alleluia!" will add to the festive spirit, and the Christmas blessing from *The Book of Occasional Services* (p. 21) concludes with the Christmas theme.

An alternative possibility for a more solemn beginning to the service is to use the Service of Light from the Order for Evening, lighting all five candles of the Advent wreath, now adorned with white candles and a Christmas bow, and substituting Gloria in excelsis or a Christmas hymn for Phos hilaron. This is also a possible beginning for the midnight eucharist.

A Christmas Vigil

The Book of Occasional Services gives direction for a vigil before the midnight eucharist. (p. 33). It begins with the Service of Light, includes additional Scripture readings "interspersed with anthems, canticles, hymns, carols, or instrumental music," and concludes with a procession to the crèche, leading into the eucharist. Its length will vary depending upon how much is read and sung. Some congregations will find it a most fitting way to prepare for their Christmas eucharist. If it is to be done, it needs to be planned well in advance, with the instrumental musicians and singers taking an active part in the planning.

"Midnight Mass"

The nighttime eucharist is, de facto, the chief Christmas service. Traditionally, the readings called "Christmas Day I" are assigned to this service. Some congregations, recognizing that few people will attend the daytime service and hear the prologue to St. John read, either use "Christmas Day III" at midnight or alternate the readings among the services over the three years of the lectionary, using John 1 every third year. The second collect, which refers to "this holy night," is obviously intended for this service. If the congregation uses both Rite One and Rite Two, the relative strengths and weaknesses of using both for the Christmas eucharist need to be weighed.

Whatever ceremonial embellishments the congregation is accustomed to use on state occasions should be used for this service: incense, golden vestments, handbells, trumpets, processional torches, banners, etc. A processional hymn with a station at the crèche makes a good beginning. Certainly a festal setting of *Gloria in excelsis* is called for. It is possible to sing the opening acclamation before it and the collect for the day after it. If this sounds festive to the parish, it can be a good idea; otherwise, it seems merely fussy. The appointed psalm can be sung (even if it is normally recited) after the Old Testament lesson and a congregational hymn, instrumental music, or a choir anthem sung after the New Testament reading, during the Gospel procession. It is important that the congregation have opportunity to sing familiar Christmas hymns, so a comprehensive plan for singing congregational hymns and choir music is helpful. If a formal Gospel procession is not a part of your usual Sunday services, this is a good occasion to introduce one.

Some congregations will feel that Christmas is an "occasion" to omit the confession of sin, to make the service more festal. Others will feel that it is important to use the confession, since there will be a number of people present who do not attend church regularly and the confession is an important part of their preparation for Christmas communion. One possibility is to use a form of the Prayers of the People (1, 5, or 6) that contains a petition for the forgiveness of sins, but some people will still consider it inadequate. There is no "correct" choice, but the discussion of whether to use the confession or not should in itself be valuable to the liturgy committee.

The Christmas proper preface states clearly the theological meaning of the festival, and it is desirable to choose a eucharistic prayer that permits its use. Eucharistic Prayer B, as we have already said, is the best choice with Rite Two. As at the earlier service, a different fraction anthem from that used during Advent will emphasize the change in season, and the more solemn form of the Christmas blessing from *The Book of Occasional Services* forms a fitting conclusion to the service.

The Twelve Days

The liturgical celebration of Christmas lasts twelve days, until the Epiphany on January 6, and includes the feasts of St. Stephen the first martyr (December 26), St. John the Apostle (December 27), the Holy Innocents murdered by Herod in his search for the Christ Child (December 28), and the Holy Name of Jesus (January 1). Only Holy Name and Epiphany are observed on Sunday. If December 26, 27, or 28 falls on Sunday, the saints' days are transferred to the following weekdays. There may be one or two Sundays after Christmas. Their services should be planned to share in as much of the Christmas festivity as possible, including liberal use of Christmas hymns and carols. *The Book of Occasional Services* contains instructions for a Christmas Festival of Lessons and Music, similar in structure to the Advent one, and this may be planned for some appropriate occasion during the twelve days.

The celebration of the twelve days is extraordinarily difficult in our culture. The "Christmas season" to most Americans begins on or before Thanksgiving and ends on

December 25. Scheduling Christmas events after Christmas seems an almost blatantly countercultural act. Holy Innocents Day (December 28) is a traditional day for a children's party. The scheduling, planning, and explaining of festive events at the church during the twelve days is one way to give reality to the season.

New Year's Day

Probably little can be done to celebrate St. Stephen, St. John, and Holy Innocents beyond scheduling a celebration of the eucharist on those days for those willing and able to attend. But a service can be planned for the New Year. January 1, now called the Holy Name of Jesus by Episcopalians and the Solemnity of Mary the Mother of God by Roman Catholics, but formerly known as the Circumcision of Christ, has probably always been observed because people felt it was good to begin the year with a church service.

The Service for New Year's Eve in *The Book of Occasional Services* is a vigil service in the classic model, consisting of lessons, psalms, and collects. If it is desired to hold such a service, it could be scheduled for 11:00 or 11:30 P.M., concluding at midnight with either the singing of the *Te Deum* or the Eucharist of the Holy Name. I know of at least one congregation that follows up a New Year's vigil and eucharist with a champagne party in the parish house. This is certainly not for every congregation, but it is a good example of imaginative planning.

Epiphany

Epiphany (January 6) is the final day of the Christmas season. It celebrates the manifestation of Christ. Its Gospel is the visit of the wise men, or magi. The baptism of Christ was originally also an Epiphany theme, and in the Eastern churches it is the primary Epiphany theme. But the present calendar commemorates the baptism on the Sunday after Epiphany. The miracle of changing water to wine at the wedding feast at Cana, now read as the Gospel on the Second Sunday after Epiphany only in Year C, is also a traditional secondary theme. Epiphany is also known as the Feast of Lights, celebrating Christ as the light of the world (John 1:5, 9). Since it is not a holiday in the United States, the only reasonable way to plan its celebration in most places is to schedule an evening eucharist. This can begin with the Service of Light from the Order for Evening, giving candles to the congregation to be lighted after the seasonal prayer for light. An Epiphany hymn with the theme of light can be substituted for the *Phos hilaron.* The Epiphany seasonal blessing concludes the service.

American Roman Catholics have given up trying to celebrate Epiphany meaningfully and transferred its celebration to the first Sunday of the new year. While insisting that the feast itself be observed on January 6, the Prayer Book does permit the use of the Epiphany Gospel on the Second Sunday after Christmas, in years when there is one. While this is not the same as celebrating Epiphany, it does give an opportunity to the congregation to hear the story of the magi.

Epiphany is the most obvious occasion for using incense in worship, since it is mentioned as a gift for the Christ Child in the Gospel. A simple way to use incense is to carry it before the Gospel book during the Gospel procession. If more extensive use is desired, the altar can be incensed after the gifts have been prepared and placed upon it. Still more extensive use would be to carry incense in the entrance and exit processions and to cense the book at the announcement of the Gospel and the congregation after the altar and gifts at the offertory. Another possibility is to burn incense in the sanctuary during the Great Thanksgiving, either instead of or in addition to carrying it in processions.

6.
The Baptism of Christ

The baptismal theme originally associated with Epiphany has been removed by the present calendar to the Sunday following, thereby greatly clarifying the planning process for both days. The Gospel in all three years of the lectionary is the baptism of Christ. The most obvious way to celebrate the day is by planning it as a parish baptismal festival. The baptismal feasts on which *The Book of Common Prayer* suggests the celebration of baptism are the Easter Vigil, Pentecost, All Saints' Day, and the Baptism of our Lord. The Easter Vigil is unique and is discussed below. On all of the remaining baptismal feasts, baptism is an appropriate highlight of the principal parish eucharist. Most of what is said in this chapter is equally applicable to the other baptismal feasts.

Planning Baptisms as Sunday Morning Worship

Baptism and its attendant rites are a cosmic event, not something to be celebrated by private appointment. The Prayer Book expects that baptisms will be celebrated "within the Eucharist as the chief service on a Sunday or other feast," and it *recommends* that they be reserved for the great baptismal feasts.

These festivals, some of the most significant in the liturgical year, are usually well planned, but often the planning does not take the baptisms into account. This is even more apt to be the case when baptisms are celebrated on other Sundays. Frequently, there is no baptismal planning at all. I have even been told in the sacristy as we were preparing to begin a service at which I was the preacher, "Oh, by the way, we're having a baptism this morning." As a result, the baptism becomes, in fact, an extra added attraction, on the level with blessing children on their birthdays, instead of the central sacramental act of rebirth and renewal in the paschal mystery that we claim it to be for both candidates and congregation.

I also continue to be shocked by discovering that there are parishes, and apparently a great many parishes, that have an admirable Sunday morning liturgy but still conduct baptism after the service, in an empty church, with no congregation but the godparents and no celebration of the eucharist. The Catechism says;

> Holy Baptism is the sacrament by which God adopts us as his children and makes us members of Christ's Body, the Church, and inheritors of the kingdom of God. . . .
>
> The inward and spiritual grace in Baptism is union with Christ in his death and resurrection, birth into God's family the Church, forgiveness of sins, and new life in the Holy Spirit.

Now, as Alexander Schmemann so aptly remarked, that is a lot of meaning for three drops of water and an empty church. If baptism, not confirmation, is the principal sacrament of Christian initiation, as the Prayer Book says it is, then we need to devote more time and energy to planning baptism than we do to planning confirmation!

If you or I were about to be incorporated into the Elks or the volunteer fire department or the Eastern Star, we would expect the whole organization to turn out company front for the event. And that, in fact, is the way most membership organizations behave. Initiations are the high spot of the year. So they always have been for the Christian Church, too. That's what Easter and the Great Vigil are all about. They are the climax of the period of preparation in which the Church initiates her new members. They and we and Christ have the right to expect the best from the liturgy team: priest, deacon, acolytes, choir, and professional or semiprofessional musicians.

"It is a matter of experience," says Fr. J.D. Crichton, an English Roman Catholic parish priest and editor of the journal *Life and Worship*, "that the sacraments, when celebrated as they should be by a believing community, draw the nonbeliever to the Church and dispose him to listen or come again. We all know that a bad celebration of the sacraments can repel people, sometimes forever." (*Christian Celebration: The Sacraments*, p. 14)

Not only do the rites of Christian initiation deserve the best presentation we can give them, which, incidentally, includes good music, but they are an unparalleled opportunity for what the Church calls evangelism and what Madison Avenue calls advertising. People who come to the baptism of a friend, or a friend's child, do not usually come prepared to be critical of either the service or the congregation.

A poorly done baptism may convince unchurched friends of the candidates that they are delighted about nothing so much as that they do not have to go back to that church again the next Sunday, while a well-done liturgy may open the door to a new pastoral relationship.

Guidelines for Baptisms

What then is required in the way of planning? First there is general planning: the setting of standards for the celebration of baptism in the parish.

Will baptisms normally be celebrated only at the great baptismal feasts, or are they regularly arranged on other Sundays? Many parishes publicize the fact that baptisms are regularly celebrated on the baptismal feasts and actively encourage scheduling them on those occasions. If baptisms are scheduled on other Sundays, care needs to be taken that they do not occur so frequently that they lose their significance. Few parishes would need to have more than one baptismal Sunday a month. We clergy need to stop thinking of baptism as a pastoral office to be scheduled for individual candidates and begin planning major baptismal occasions with our liturgy committees at which several candidates will be presented.

What provision is made for the preparation of parents and godparents (*BCP*, p. 298)? Regular sessions should be scheduled before baptismal days.

When are adult candidates for baptism presented? The best times are the Easter Vigil, particularly if a formal catechumenate can be established during Lent (as provided in *The Book of Occasional Services*), and at the bishop's visitation, when the bishop can baptize, anoint, and lay hands on them.

Frequently, these guidelines are approved by the vestry and published for the information of parents and adult candidates. Often information about forthcoming baptismal days is regularly included in the Sunday bulletin. The worship or liturgy committee should work with the rector to prepare the guidelines and help in "selling" them to the vestry and to the congregation. The formal approval of the guidelines by the vestry will make them "parish policy" and involve the parish in understanding and approving what is being done. Their publication will make it clear that everyone has the same rules, and individuals are not being singled out for preferential or discriminatory treatment.

Planning the Services

The services themselves need to be carefully planned. If the candidates are infants, will they be present during the liturgy of the Word or brought in from the nursery after the sermon, immediately before the presentation of the candidates? What plans need to be made to permit other children in the congregation to see and hear the baptism?

The sermon should relate to the baptism. This is easy to do on the great baptismal feasts. The Baptism of Christ is the principal theme this Sunday, and the homilist may move from Christ's baptism directly to our participation in Christ through baptism. On the other baptismal feasts, different aspects of baptism are emphasized, and they are the basis for including the baptisms being held that day in the sermon. On ordinary Sundays, you may wish to take advantage of the permission given (*BCP*, p. 312) to substitute one of the lessons "at Baptism" for one of the lessons of the day to make it easier to make the connections. The Prayer Book suggests that sponsors might read the lessons, and this can be included in the planning of the service.

If the font is located in a place that makes it difficult for the congregation to participate, the entire first part of the service can be conducted from the chancel step with a procession to the font immediately before the Thanksgiving over the Water and (if necessary) a return to the front of the church between the baptism and consignation. Ideally, the celebrant should stand to face the congregation across the font, and the baptismal parties should be placed so as to include, rather than exclude, the congregation in the action. All of this needs to be worked out beforehand.

The Peace includes the welcome of the newly baptized. Not just the clergy, but members of the vestry and the liturgy committee should make it a point to greet the newly baptized, their parents, and sponsors. Other parishioners will follow their lead and welcome the new Christians.

After the exchange of the Peace, the service continues "with the Prayers of the People or the Offertory of the Eucharist." Continuing with the Prayers of the People is often awkward, since the Peace has already been exchanged. One way to avoid it is to move directly to the offertory and include necessary intercessions in Eucharistic Prayer D. The Prayer Book recommends that newly baptized adults, or the godparents of newly baptized infants, bring up the bread and wine at the offertory.

Music for Baptisms

Music is a principal area in which the importance of the baptism can be reflected and one that requires careful planning. Hymns must be chosen with care. Baptism is an Easter experience, and this can be reflected in the hymns. There are some good hymns for baptism in *The Hymnal 1982*. If the candidates are adults, a whole other group of hymns speaking of commitment to Christ (such as "St. Patrick's Breastplate") become available.

The singing of responsorial psalms, such as those in the *Gradual Psalms*, or congregational hymns between the readings can help to turn a wordy monologue into a corporate act of worship. This is equally true for regular Sunday eucharists, but baptismal days might be an occasion to introduce the practice if your congregation does not already use music in this part of the service.

After the Baptismal Covenant, the Prayers for the Candidates may be sung. I would not want to see it done always and everywhere, but places where the Litany is regularly sung in procession on the Sundays in Lent should have no difficulty in singing the Prayers for the Candidates during the procession to the font. Alternatively, the Prayers for the Candidates may be said by a godparent and a baptismal hymn or, as the Prayer Book recommends, Psalm 42 sung during the procession. Personally, I have found this a good point for a hymn in most parishes—or even a metrical setting of the psalm. Of course, if the font is located in a place where everyone can see the baptism, the Presentation and Examination of the Candidates and the Baptismal Covenant can take place at the font, and there is no need for a procession. It might still be desirable to ask children who cannot see over the heads of adult members of the congregation to come and stand around the font at this time and to sing a hymn to cover the chaos of their movement.

The Altar Book contains music for the Thanksgiving over the Water, and certainly this can be sung on at least the major baptismal feasts in any parish and by any priest who was accustomed to sing the eucharistic prefaces. Music is also provided for the Consecration of Chrism for the bishop's use when consecrating chrism as a part of the baptismal liturgy. But whether the bishop can and will sing it is beyond the power of recommendation of most parish worship committees. The Prayer Book also suggests Psalm 23 for the procession from the baptistry after the baptism, if one is necessary so that the people can see the signing with the cross. Even if no procession is necessary, it may be desirable to create a "break" after the actual baptisms so that baptismal parties can regroup and children return to their seats. I have found that "The King of Love" or one of the other metrical settings to the Shepherd Psalm goes very well. The words are theologically significant in the context of washing with water, anointing with oil, and feeding at the Lord's Table, and the tunes strong and singable.

Certainly it would be a great boon on these occasions, as well as at weddings, funerals, and other potentially ecumenical occasions, if everyone who uses the ecumenical ICET text of the liturgy (that's Roman Catholics, Episcopalians, Lutherans, Methodists, and Presbyterians for starters) learned at least one common setting for the eucharist. There should be enough common music that we can all join together in a baptismal or funeral or wedding liturgy, singing music that is already familiar to us all. Failing that, it would be helpful at the very least to get all of the episcopal churches in the same diocese to learn a common setting! This is something a parish could easily recommend to its diocesan liturgy and music commission.

In general, the details of the service need to be planned as carefully as those of the Christmas or Easter services. Baptisms are important occasions not only for the candidates, their families, and friends but for the entire parish, whose life in the Body of Christ is renewed whenever we celebrate the paschal sacrament of new birth. They deserve the very best we can offer.

If There Are No Baptisms

Occasionally there will be a baptismal feast for which there are, in fact, no baptisms in a given congregation. Advance publicity and planning can reduce the likelihood of this happening, but it will sometimes happen. On all of the baptismal feasts, the congregation can renew their own baptismal vows in place of reciting the Nicene Creed (*BCP*, 312). The form included in the Prayer Book for the Easter Vigil (p. 292) is used. A brief introduction, comparable to that given for Easter, can be composed to introduce the renewal, or it can follow the sermon directly, the sermon itself serving as an introduction and explanation.

The Baptism of Christ

Whether or not there are baptisms, baptism is clearly the central theme for this service. The proper preface may be of the Epiphany or the Lord's Day. Lord's Day 3 refers to our being made a new people in Jesus Christ "by water and the Holy Spirit" and appears to be the best choice. If Eucharistic Prayer D is used, there is no proper preface. The liturgical color for the day is white, and the service music used during the Christmas season can be continued through this Sunday, although (if there are baptisms) the *Gloria in excelsis* is not needed. The Epiphany seasonal blessing is also used on this Sunday.

7.
Planning for Lent

Lent is the one season for which most parishes do plan. It needs to be planned in its totality. Before inviting guest preachers or working on individual special events, attention needs to be given to an overall seasonal plan, including the Sunday eucharists, weekday services, Ash Wednesday, Holy Week, and any special services or programs to be added to the calendar. The pamphlet *Celebrating Redemption: The Liturgies of Lent, Holy Week, and the Great Fifty Days* from Associated Parishes is an excellent resource.

Lent

The inner meaning of Lent is well described in the special liturgy for Ash Wednesday:

> [The] season of Lent provided a time in which converts to the faith were prepared for Holy Baptism. It was also a time when those who, because of notorious sins, had been separated from the body of the faithful were reconciled by penitence and forgiveness, and restored to the fellowship of the Church. Thereby, the whole congregation was put in mind of the message of pardon set forth in the Gospel of our Savior, and of the need which all Christians continually have to renew their repentance and faith. (*BCP*, p. 264f)

Preparation of candidates for baptism at the Great Vigil of Easter, then, is the primary purpose of Lent, and if there will be catechumens preparing for Easter baptism, then this is the first consideration in Lenten planning. What is necessary for the formation of new members is generally also what is necessary for the renewal of those whose initial ardor has somewhat cooled. A program designed for catechumens will often be the same program needed for parish Lenten renewal.

Lent is also a season of repentance and renewal for the

whole congregation. The same exhortation in the Ash Wednesday liturgy suggests self-examination and repentance; prayer, fasting, and self-denial; and reading and meditating on God's holy Word as the means to a holy Lent. Further suggestions are found in the second Lenten preface:

> You bid your faithful people cleanse their hearts, and prepare with joy for the Paschal feast; that, fervent in prayer and in works of mercy, and renewed by your Word and Sacraments, they may come to the fullness of grace which you have prepared for those who love you. (BCP, p. 379)

The Prayer Book has given us a master plan for our Lenten observances and a suggestion of the elements to be included. The mention of joy in the preface is most important. Reginald Fuller has publicly commented that, while Ash Wednesday is indeed a sort of Christian *Yom Kippur*, we are not supposed to turn the forty days of Lent into forty consecutive *Yomim Kippurim*. Joy and renewal by Word and sacrament are as important as prayer, fasting, and self-denial in the overall planning.

Planning This Lent

What then are the elements we need to consider for this Lent? Many of these are, of course, specific to your particular congregation, and no one, including a rector who has just arrived, can tell you what they are. The attempt to do global planning usually results in irrelevant programs and bored congregations. But there are a number of common elements and some questions we all need to ask.

The propers for the three years of the liturgical lectionary are quite different. It is important to plan for *this* year. In Years A and C, for example, the propers for the First Sunday in Lent focus on the temptation of Christ in the wilderness. In Year B they talk about the flood and the baptism of Christ, with only a passing reference to the temptation in the wilderness. It is appropriate to sing "Forty days and forty nights" on this Sunday in Years A and C, but to sing it in Year B misses the major themes of the propers.

The Lenten Sundays of Year A contain the ancient Gospels for the preparation of catechumens for Easter baptism, the great Johannine "signs of the Kingdom." Lent 2 of this year has John 3, the discussion with Nicodemus on being born again. Lent 3 tells the story of the woman at the well of Samaria. Lent 4 gives us the miracle of the man born blind who was healed by washing in the pool of Siloam. And Lent 5 provides the climax of the series with the raising of Lazarus. Whether or not there are adult candidates preparing for Easter baptism, this series of Gospels demands serious consideration in planning both hymns and sermons.

In Year B, Lent 2 gives us the binding of Isaac and the rebuke of Peter, with the call to deny yourself and take up the cross. Perhaps this is an opportunity to introduce the hymn "Lift high the Cross" (hymn 475). Lent 3 features the decalogue and the cleansing of the Temple. Is this an occasion to use the Ten Commandments? The propers for Lent 4 include Ephesians 2 on salvation by grace through faith and the Johannine account of the feeding of the five thousand. This is the year in which Lent 4 retains its "Refreshment Sunday" theme. This year, but not in Years A and C, this can be a part of plans for the day. Lent 5 offers us the new covenant from Jeremiah, Psalm 51 (the *Miserere*), Hebrews 5 on Christ the high priest, and John 12, concluding, "When I am lifted up from the earth, I will draw everyone to me." This is the theme of a new hymn, "When Christ was lifted from the earth" (hymn 603), which could be introduced. It is important that these powerful themes be treated as a group, leading naturally to the Markan Passion on the following Sunday of the Passion.

Year C produces a different set of themes. After the temptation on Lent 1, Lent 2 has the covenant with Abraham from Genesis 15, an eschatological passage from Philippians 3, and the Lukan Gospel about the hen gathering her chickens about her. Lent 3 has the burning bush (Exodus 3), and a Gospel (Luke 13:1-9) that combines the parable of the fig tree with the question of why natural disasters befall some people rather than others. Lent 4 tells the story of the prodigal son, and Lent 5 the parable of the vineyard. All of these provide significant Lenten themes but probably not as obviously as the other two years.

Sermon themes, hymns, anthems, and programs can be integrated, *if we start thinking about it early enough*. It is especially important to think about the unity of the Sunday services if the same priest will not be preacher or celebrant every Sunday, as is more likely to be true in Lent than in other seasons in many parishes. It is especially important that the parish musicians understand and have a share in planning the themes for the services and other events of which music is an integral part, so that the music may contribute to the service, not compete with it.

A Lenten "Look" for the Church Building

The use of a well-designed Lenten array can strikingly alter the interior appearance of the church and really mark Lent as a "different" season. The Sarum Lenten array, off-white or "unbleached linen" vestments and frontal with matching veils for crosses and statues, is increasingly being used in place of violet during Lent. There is no theological implication in using one or the other. It is a matter of taste and personal preference. A special Lenten processional cross may also be used—wood painted red with black edges is traditional, or the usual cross can be veiled. The use of red for Palm Sunday and the other days of Holy Week, incidentally, is both the old Sarum and new Roman custom and has much to commend it. Sarum Holy Week vestments tend toward the oxblood in color with black orphreys and have the advantage of not appearing to be festal. Whatever is actually done, planning for Lent should include ways to mark the season in the adornment of the church building as one more way to call the people's attention to the season.

Selecting the Options

Many parishes appear to have made a policy decision that "during Lent we do Rite One." This may be a reasonable decision, but it should be rethought each Lent. It may, among other things, be grossly unfair to Rite One, which will become associated in the minds of the congregation with Lent and penitence. Eucharistic Prayers A and C of Rite Two are eminently suitable for Lenten use and can be considered as possibilities. *The Hymnal 1982* contains at least one excellent musical setting for Rite Two suitable for Lent because of its relative simplicity, David Hurd's "New Plainsong" (S 86, S 100, S 124, S 161).

Obvious choices for Lenten Sundays are the use of the Penitential Order at the beginning of the liturgy or the substitution of the Great Litany for all that precedes the collect. The Great Litany may be sung in procession to the music at S 67 in *The Hymnal 1982* or sung or recited from a litany desk at the front of the nave or sung "in the midst of the choir." It need not be led by a priest, and it is often desirable for a member of the choir to do so. Not only may this be musically preferable, it gives a lay member of the congregation another opportunity to take a prominent role in the leadership of the Sunday service. In any case, the celebrant says or sings "The Lord be with you" and the collect. If the Great Litany is used, the Prayers of the People are appropriately omitted. *Gloria in excelsis*, of course, is not used in Lent.

Another option worth considering is the use of canticle 14, "A Song of Penitence" (*Kyrie Pantokrator*), in either a plainsong or Anglican chant setting. (S 237–S 241). The singing of the canticle may accompany the entrance procession, in place of the entrance hymn, possibly with the Penitential Order following. Using this penitential canticle at the beginning of the service sets a definite Lenten tone for the eucharist. Alternatively, the *Kyrie Pantokrator* can be used between the New Testament reading and the Gospel.

Simple musical settings for the psalms to be sung between the first two lessons are found in *Gradual Psalms*, as mentioned in chapter 2. The pages are scored for easy removal, and purchase of a copy includes permission to reproduce them for the Sunday bulletin. A change in the method of treating the gradual psalm is another way to mark a distinct season. Other methods of doing the psalm are given in chapter 2.

Traditionally, Alleluia is not sung during Lent, and *Gradual Psalms* includes a *Tract*, that is, psalm verses to be sung straight through without refrain or antiphon, to be used in place of an Alleluia verse between the New Testament lesson and Gospel. The settings of the Tracts in *Gradual Psalms* can easily be done by a cantor or small choir. These traditional selections may be used, or a hymn or canticle may be sung. One possibility is to use the same short congregational response, such as a single hymn or psalm verse, every Sunday as a mark of the season.

The Litany of Penitence from the Ash Wednesday liturgy (*BCP*, p. 267ff) can be used on one or more Sundays in place of the Confession of Sin. It "may be preceded by an appropriate invitation and a penitential psalm" (*BCP*, p. 269). If it is used on the First Sunday in Lent, the last paragraph of the Ash Wednesday invitation is appropriate. (*BCP*, p. 265). For other Sundays, it can be easily adapted. To combine this option with the Great Litany at the beginning of the service, the recitation of the Decalogue, or the Penitential Order will almost certainly result in liturgical "overkill." Even in penitence, less is often more.

Serious consideration should be given to using the second of the two alternative proper prefaces, except on the First Sunday in Years A and C when the temptation in the wilderness is the Gospel theme. Eucharistic Prayer I in Rite One and A and C in Rite Two seem most appropriate for Lenten use. Which one you actually choose will depend largely on the style of liturgy to which your congregation is accustomed. The rector, of course, has the canonical right to decide, but the involvement of others (curates, deacons, lay readers, musicians, worshipers) in the decision will give all a feeling of "ownership" of the planned services.

During Lent, the *Agnus Dei* may be sung in place of the anthem "Christ our Passover" at the fraction. Or one of the proper *confractoria*, or fraction anthems, given in *The Book of Occasional Services* may be used. *Confractorium 6*, "Whoever believes in me shall not hunger or thirst, for the bread which I give for the life of the world is my flesh," is appropriate for Lent 4 in Year B. Music for many of these fraction anthems is included in *The Hymnal 1982*. A setting of this one is at S 170, but many local musicians are interested in setting liturgical texts for their own choirs. Using a setting composed locally increases the sense of it being "our" liturgy.

The Book of Occasional Services contains a collection of solemn Prayers over the People that may be used in place of a seasonal blessing during Lent. Six numbered prayers and one intended for use from Palm Sunday through Maundy Thursday are included. The first may be used on Ash Wednesday and the next five on the Sundays in Lent. On the weekdays, the prayer from the previous Sunday may be used, or, if there is a daily celebration, a different one of the six prayers may be used every day. The deacon, or celebrant, introduces the prayer with "Bow down before the Lord." This is an invitation to the congregation to kneel or at least bow. The celebrant may extend both arms toward the congregation while saying (or singing) the prayer. Like the seasonal blessings, these prayers are completely optional. They are printed in *The Book of Occasional Services* (p. 22ff) in contemporary language. But, following the general rubric on page 14 of *The Book of Common Prayer*, "the contemporary idiom may be conformed to traditional language" for use in Rite One services.

Ash Wednesday

The first day of Lent has its own special liturgy. The Ash Wednesday liturgy is the first of the Proper Liturgies for Special Days in *The Book of Common Prayer* (pp. 264–69). Since it is held only once a year, it requires not only planning but rehearsal if it is to be well done. The planning committee members can often help their successors by making notes about particular problems and, we hope, solutions for special liturgies such as this. This does not mean that the parish liturgy committee should simply look at the notes from last year's service and decide to do it again. Much of it may deserve repetition, some things can doubtless be improved, and other things the committee may simply choose to do differently.

Since Ash Wednesday is normally a working day for most people, the principal liturgy needs to be scheduled at an hour when most parishioners will be able to come. This usually means in the evening. At least one other service will be necessary in most congregations, and in many both an early morning and midday service will be helpful. The Prayer Book expects the principal service to be a eucharist, and many parishes will celebrate the eucharist at all services on this day. A public celebration of the office with a homily after the second reading is a good alternative for at least one service. Morning Prayer with a Lenten opening sentence, the Confession of Sin, Psalm 95 instead of the *Venite*, and *Kyrie Pantokrator* (canticle 14) and *Benedictus* (canticle 16) as the canticles provides a bracing beginning for the day and the season.

The ceremony that gave its name to the day, the imposition of ashes, is an optional part of the proper Ash Wednesday liturgy. The form on page 265 of the Prayer Book could also be used to impose ashes on other occasions during the day, such as after the anthem at the daily office.

Ash Wednesday is a day of fasting and penitence, and its liturgy has an austere quality. It begins with "The Lord be with you" and the collect of the day, without any entrance rite. The singing of an entrance hymn is not actually forbidden, but entering in silence is certainly a reasonable option. If it is desired to sing something during the entrance of the (choir and) ministers, the canticle *Kyrie Pantokrator*, suggested above for other occasions in Lent, is suitable.

The special ceremonies take place after the sermon. "[T]he Celebrant or Minister appointed invites the people to the observance of a holy Lent" (*BCP*, p. 264). The word *Minister* here and in other prayer book rubrics does not imply that the person is ordained. It is a technical term for the major assistants at liturgical functions. The celebrant, another priest or deacon, or a lay reader may issue the invitation, reading the form in the Prayer Book. It would be interesting to consider the effect of having this invitation read by a churchwarden or other lay leader of the congregation. Lay people are accustomed to hearing the clergy tell them to pray fast and deny themselves.

Following the invitation, the congregation kneels in the silence, and ashes may be imposed. It is not clear whether Psalm 51 (*Miserere*) is to be sung during the imposition or at its conclusion. If it is to be said, it must certainly follow the imposition, but, if the choir would like to sing the psalm, either to a chant or an anthem setting during the imposition of ashes, it could be quite effective. All of these possibilities can be considered by the planning committee.

Special Lenten Observances

Once the Ash Wednesday and Sunday liturgies are planned, then decisions about extra Lenten services, guest preachers, the Presiding Bishop's Fund for World Relief, and all of the local Lenten concerns are in order. The total Lenten program may present a unified theme rooted in the liturgical readings for the Sundays, or there may be other themes in harmony or counterpoint to the main theme, as long as there are not discordant or competing themes.

Many parishes have a midweek evening service during Lent, either introducing an evening program or with a series of sermons. The Order of Worship for the Evening is almost ideally suited for such services of congregational common worship. There is a special Lenten prayer over the light (*BCP*, p. 111). The Lenten *Lucernarium* from *The Book of Occasional Services* (hereafter *BOS*, p. 11) is set to music in the appendix to *The Hymnal 1982*, found in the Accompaniment Edition Volume I (S 312). If the congregation's resources include a good cantor to lead the people in singing it, consider using it. But it is completely optional, and the candles may be lighted in silence, and then either *Phos hilaron* or an appropriate Lenten hymn, such as "Kind maker of the world," the medieval office hymn (hymn 152), sung. The intention of the service is that the music be congregational, not a cathedral-like performance by a choir, so singability and familiarity are important criteria for deciding what to use. The *Magnificat* may be sung to a plainsong or Anglican chant from the Hymnal or to a metrical setting. The excellent metrical setting to the Song of Simeon (*Nunc Dimittis*) by Rae E. Whitney, "Lord God, you now have set your servant free," is set in the Hymnal to Orlando Gibbons' *Song 1* (hymn 499) and will be sung with joy by most congregations. It is not necessary to use the Evening Prayer psalm and lesson for the weekday on which the service happens to be held. The daily office lectionary was intended for course reading. An appropriate lesson from the previous Sunday or any day during the way can and should be chosen. The same choice is available for a psalm, or one of the evening psalms mentioned on page 143 of the Prayer Book may be used.

Sometimes nonliturgical services of various kinds are held or parish suppers and educational programs. The Way of the Cross (*BOS*, pp. 54–71) may be held on Fridays during Lent. The important thing is not so much the decisions that any particular parish makes in its Lenten planning but that there be planning and that *some* decisions that make sense in the worshiping life of that parish be made.

Preparing for Easter Baptism

The enrollment of candidates for Easter baptism traditionally takes place on the First Sunday in Lent. After the creed, the catechumens who are to be enrolled as candidates come forward with their sponsors. The sponsors are queried about the *bona fides* of the catechumens, and the congregation is asked if it approves of their being enrolled. The enrollment itself involves the candidates writing their names in a large book. This is followed by a litany led by the deacon (if there is one) and a blessing of the candidates by the celebrant. On the other Sundays in Lent, the candidates are prayed for by name, and special prayers may be said over the candidates on the Third, Fourth, and Fifth Sundays. These rites are for unbaptized candidates going through the catechumenate and are contained in *The Book of Occasional Services.* All of this will require serious planning, especially if it has never been done before in the congregation.

In addition to these rites for catechumens, *The Book of Occasional Services,* 2d edition, contains the "Preparation of Baptized Persons for Reaffirmation of the Baptismal Covenant," authorized by the 1988 General Convention (*BOS*, pp. 132–41). This is a program, parallel to the catechumenate, for those already baptized. It involves "The Calling of the Baptized to Continuing Conversion" at the principal liturgy on Ash Wednesday, a period during Lent when the candidates for reaffirmation "focus on the Lenten disciplines and their role in ministry to others. . . . share their on-going experience of conversion. . . . and explore more deeply the life of prayer and ministry," and a Maundy Thursday rite of preparation for their reaffirmation of baptismal vows at the Paschal Vigil.

Obviously, if the catechumenate is in use in the parish, these programs need to form an important part of the observance of Lent. But even if there are no catechumens or adult candidates for reaffirmation, the liturgical planning committee does well to look at all of this material, for these are the themes of Lent itself, and an understanding of them can be useful in planning a more general overall parish Lenten program.

8.
Planning for Holy Week

That Holy Week is the heart and center of the liturgical year is beyond dispute. Theologically and liturgically, if not in practice, the Great Vigil of Easter is the central service of the Church Year, and the principal liturgies of Maundy Thursday and Good Friday are closely related to it. They demand, and usually receive, our best efforts. Every parish *plans* its Holy Week observances, but many are disappointed in the results. Palm Sunday and Easter are high points, but often the rest of the week does not fulfill the hopes and expectations of the planners. Both planning and rehearsal of what has been planned are necessary. Before the first rehearsal is held, all the decisions about what is to be done should already have been made.

Technically, Holy Week planning could be considered a part of Lenten planning. But not only is Holy Week really distinct from the rest of Lent, it is practically a good idea to have a different subcommittee or commission of your liturgical planning committee plan it. The broader the base of the planning, the better the possibilities that the services will attract the worshipers and will be within the ability of the congregation to celebrate effectively. Also, the planners and liturgical participants will have an opportunity to learn about the meaning of the paschal mystery that the Holy Week liturgies celebrate and to become missionaries and advocates to their fellow parishioners, urging them to participate in the Holy Week liturgies.

Holy Week in the Small Church

One thing that discourages many small parishes is the memory many clergy and lay people have of how magnificently the Holy Week services were celebrated in large churches with extensive musical and clerical resources. "Our little church could never hope to duplicate the splendid worship of the Great Parish in the Big City!" This is true but largely irrelevant. Liturgy in small churches is different from that in large cathedrals, just as parish life is different, and the advantages are not all on one side.

A small parish can achieve a degree of participation in its liturgies that is impossible in a large congregation. The Holy Week services can be effectively celebrated by small groups using simple music and available resources, but they must be carefully planned to encourage congregational participation and to avoid attempting to do things beyond the skills of the participants.

Getting Started

The first step in the planning is, as always, to assess the available resources. Just because something is in the Prayer Book or *The Book of Occasional Services* does not mean that it can or should be done. In most parishes it will not be realistic to plan Tenebrae for Wednesday night, a solemn Maundy Thursday eucharist, the Three Hours, the Good Friday liturgy, a Holy Saturday Word liturgy, the Great Vigil, and Easter morning as major services with "all the stops pulled out," with a eucharist on Monday, Tuesday, and Wednesday, and the Stations of the Cross at some convenient time as additional offerings. The choir director, the altar guild, and the acolytes can help the parish to set a reasonable course. The special liturgies of Maundy Thursday, Good Friday, and the Great Vigil should be the primary foci.

Decide what services will be held. Start with the Liturgy of the Palms on Palm Sunday, the Maundy Thursday eucharist, the Good Friday liturgy, and as solemn an Easter eucharist as the traditions and resources of the parish permit. Then give serious thought to the Great Vigil. We shall consider planning for the Great Vigil and Easter Day in the next chapter.

Palm Sunday

Palm Sunday has a double title in *The Book of Common Prayer* that accurately expresses the nature of the day: "The

Sunday of the Passion: Palm Sunday." The blessing of the palms and the triumphal procession modulate into a penitential eucharist dominated by the Gospel account of the crucifixion. The two themes are quite distinct and cannot be mixed.

The Prayer Book, the Altar Book and *The Hymnal 1982* provide the necessary texts and music. The music for the Liturgy of the Palms is at hymns 153–57. Holy Week red is usually used today as the liturgical color. If copes are worn in the parish, the celebrant may wear one for the palm liturgy. The palms can be set out in the parish hall or some other appropriate place outside the church. If this is not possible, they may be placed at the church door and blessed there. The opening anthem may be sung or said as a versicle and response. The parish deacon, if there is one, reads the Gospel at the Liturgy of the Palms. The reading may be accompanied by the ceremonial customary at the Sunday eucharist. In the absence of a deacon, another priest may read the Gospel, or it may be read as a lesson by a layperson without the Gospel ceremonies. The blessing itself may be sung in the same way as the eucharistic preface. The music for the responses is in the Hymnal and that for the celebrant's part in *The Altar Book*. No particular ceremonial actions are necessary, but a sign of the cross may be made over the branches at "Let these branches be for us . . .," and they may be sprinkled with holy water and incensed at the conclusion of the prayer. The clergy, acolytes, and ushers all assist in distributing the palms as expeditiously as possible. If it is desired to simplify the ceremony and reduce the time, the palms may be distributed by the ushers as people arrive and then held up to be blessed at the appropriate time.

The palm procession need not involve thurifers, banners, torches, and many clergy, although they are all appropriate when they are available. Carrying the palm branches in procession into the church in celebration of Christ's triumphal entry into Jerusalem is the reason for blessing the palms, so the procession should be impressive and involve all of the congregation able to participate. The traditional music for the procession is the hymn "All glory, laud, and honor" (hymn 154/155). The verses may be sung by the choir, or groups within the choir, with the congregation joining in the refrain. Ps. 118:19–29 (hymn 157) has an even longer association with the Palm Sunday procession, being quoted in the biblical account. An effective way to use both is to have the choir (or cantors) sing the verses of the psalm, with everyone joining in the antiphon, beginning the hymn when the procession enters the church. The psalm can be sung a capella or with hand bells ringing the intervals, the organ accompanying the hymn.

The concluding collect of the procession marks the distinct change in theme from "Palm Sunday" to "The Sunday of the Passion." Hymns or anthems with the triumphal entry as their theme belong at the palm liturgy, while music during the eucharist reflects the passion theme. "Ride on! ride on in majesty!" (hymn 156), for example, can be used as an additional hymn during the procession, while "O sacred head" (hymn 169) is more appropriate at the offertory or the end of the service. Other "suitable anthems" may replace the opening anthem of the Liturgy of the Palms from the Prayer Book or be sung during the distribution of palms. If the choir wishes to sing a Palm Sunday anthem, either of these places is suitable.

The passion Gospel is the distinctive element of the eucharist itself. It may be read responsively or sung. Mason Martens has published settings of the traditional music to the Revised Standard Version texts. (New York: Music for Liturgy) Many parishes enjoy reading the Passion dramatically, with the congregation taking the part of the crowd. Readers for the Passion can be recruited from the choir or congregation. The priest may simply listen or take the part of Jesus.

If there is an early service on Palm Sunday, be sure to plan some form of palm liturgy for it. A simple form would be to have the congregation hold their palms for the Gospel and blessing, and then sing "All glory, laud, and honor" (hymn 154) while the altar party processes to the sanctuary.

Although a small congregation can do this for their main Palm Sunday liturgy, most congregations will wish to do more. The congregation gathers in the parish house or even in the narthex. The opening anthem can be said, or the choir may lead its singing. The collect, Gospel, and blessing of the palms may be said by the priest, and the *Benedictus qui venit* sung to any familiar tune. All enter the church, led by the crucifer, singing "All glory, laud, and honor" and concluding with the collect said before the altar.

Maundy Thursday

The Maundy Thursday liturgy is properly a Holy Week service, the only eucharist celebrated between Wednesday and the Great Vigil. Many parishes wish to emphasize this setting, using Holy Week red vestments, while others make it a festal celebration for the institution of the eucharist, a sort of Corpus Christi. Either emphasis is possible, but it should be carried through consistently.

The Prayer Book provides for the "maundy," or foot washing. This requires a good deal of planning. How many people will have their feet washed? Will they be chosen representatives, or should all who wish to come forward be invited to do so? People need advance instruction about what to wear so that they will not be embarrassed. Lay members of the planning committee can be particularly helpful in setting this up. Hymn 576 ("God is love"), hymn 606 ("Where charity and love dwell"), or settings of the anthems given on pages 274-75 in the Prayer Book (such as those at S 344-S 347 in the Appendix to the Accompaniment Edition of *The Hymnal 1982*) are appropriately sung during the washing. It is worth considering asking the churchwardens, or other significant lay leaders of the parish, to join the rector in washing the feet of the parishioners.

Reserving the sacrament for Good Friday communion is not contingent upon having an altar of repose and keeping a watch. A parish that does not wish to introduce these customs may simply reserve the sacrament in both kinds in some convenient place, such as a chapel or the sacristy, from which it can be brought before communion in the Good Friday liturgy. The priest or deacon may simply take the sacrament to this place after communion without ceremony. Other parishes will wish to carry the sacrament solemnly to an altar of repose, with lights, incense, and to the accompaniment of music (hymn 329-30 and 331, "Now, my tongue the mystery telling" is traditional). A "watch" may be kept here until the Good Friday liturgy. Matt. 26:40-41, "Could you not watch with me one hour? Watch and pray that you may not enter into temptation . . . ," is usually given as the biblical warrant. In some places, a prayer vigil is kept instead from the end of the Good Friday liturgy to the beginning of the Easter Vigil, imitating the watch set before the tomb. Whether or not your congregation does either of these, it is certainly appropriate to encourage people to come to the church to pray during the period between Maundy Thursday and Easter. If the church is not usually left open, this can require a little planning and someone to watch the property, if not to watch before the Lord.

Good Friday

The proper liturgy should be the principal Good Friday service. The time of day it is held will depend on the convenience of the parish. The Good Friday liturgy as the solemn corporate commemoration of the great events of the day does not lend itself to being repeated. If it is necessary to have a second Good Friday service, one of the offices with a sermon or meditation, or the Way of the Cross, is often a good choice.

The Good Friday liturgy is not a funeral for Jesus. Its theme is epitomized in the refrain to Anthem 1 for the veneration of the cross:

We glory in your cross, O Lord,
and praise and magnify your holy resurrection;
for by virtue of your cross
joy has come to the whole world.
(*BCP*, p. 281)

The older custom of wearing black vestments on Good Friday has largely been replaced by the use of red for the king of martyrs. The celebrant may wear a cope, alb (or surplice) and stole, or eucharistic vestments. Assisting clergy and acolytes wear their usual vestments, albs or cassock and surplice. The custom of wearing a black cassock without a surplice on this day derives from the recognition that the Three Hours is not a liturgical service. Therefore the clergy do not vest, but wear only the cassock, their "street clothes." This custom does not make sense when followed at the liturgy.

The liturgy begins with a silent entrance, a distinctive salutation, and the collect of the day. It is highly desirable to use all three readings and the psalm between the Old Testament lesson and the epistle. The St. John Passion may be read dramatically or sung. It may be desirable to handle it differently from the synoptic Passion on Palm Sunday. Whatever decision is made, both for today and Palm Sunday, the purpose is to proclaim Christ crucified, not to have a beautiful experience. The sermon follows the Passion immediately and is obviously a major proclamation of the day's theme.

The Solemn Collects are Prayers of the People. Whether they are sung or said, the pattern is for a deacon or layperson to bid the prayers of the congregation, then after a pause for prayer, the celebrant prays the collect. The ancient tradition was to have the bidder invite the people to kneel after each bidding and then, after their silent prayer, invite them to stand for the collect. This really does involve a lot of getting up and down. Many, probably most, congregations direct the people either to stand or to kneel throughout the Solemn Collects.

For the Veneration of the Cross, three anthems are given in the Prayer Book, which could be recited or sung to appropriate music (the Hymnal appendix, S 349–S 351). The Reproaches, which disappeared from *The Draft Proposed Book of Common Prayer* during the debate at the 1976 General Convention, may also be sung, and music is readily available. A revised version of the text is found in the Canadian *Book of Alternative Services*. The suggested hymn, "Sing, my tongue the glorious battle," is found at hymns 165 and 166 in *The Hymnal 1982* and at S 352 in the appendix. The recitation or singing of the anthems—and the singing of the hymn as the congregation kneels before a large wooden cross—is devotionally effective and unlikely to be as upsetting to some people as various methods of coming forward to venerate a cross or crucifix. This entire portion of the liturgy is optional, and the service may end after the Solemn Collects with the concluding prayer.

If communion is to be administered, the sacrament is brought simply to the altar, the confession said, and communion administered in the usual way, making use of the customary ministers of communion. The altar is stripped after communion and, following the single prayer given in the Prayer Book, the altar party leaves in silence.

Other Services

These are the principal Holy Week services to which you should devote your primary resources. Then plan other services within the congregation's ability to participate. In planning for Holy Week, it is better to consider the needs of the congregation as a whole, and to plan corporate services for congregational participation, than to provide a smorgasbord to meet the varying devotional needs of many individuals.

Other services include eucharists for Monday, Tuesday, and Wednesday, and a Word liturgy for Holy Saturday. These may follow the congregation's usual customs for weekday services and be scheduled for any convenient hour. The Word liturgy for Holy Saturday is quite brief and is a convenient service for those about to prepare the church for Easter to celebrate together. The daily offices may also be celebrated. However tempting it may be to schedule all of the above, it is important not to offer so many services that none is well attended and everyone feels guilty, exhausted, or both.

The Three Hours is a nonliturgical service of preaching of the Passion, interspersed with hymns, prayers, and periods of silence, held between noon and 3 P.M. on Good Friday. It is of South American Jesuit origin. It became, nevertheless, the usual Good Friday service for both Catholics and Protestants until the liturgical reforms of the last half of the twentieth century. Today it is often an ecumenical service in a downtown church. Few congregations will wish to introduce such a service, but many will find it in place and well attended. In your liturgical planning, avoid conflicting with it when scheduling the Good Friday liturgy.

The Way (or Stations) of the Cross, a medieval devotion supposedly brought back from the Crusades by Francis of Assisi, is a good "second service" for Good Friday. It is in *The Book of Occasional Services* (pp. 54–71), and alternative forms are readily available. It can be adapted as a children's service or an outdoor service or both. The procession can also be omitted and the format used for a series of devotional addresses.

9.
Planning for Easter and the Great Fifty Days

The Great Vigil of Easter celebrates our Lord's passage from death to life and our participation in that victory through the paschal mystery. The sacraments of baptism and eucharist are both the signs and the means of this participation, for in the Easter sacraments we go down into the grave with Christ and are raised with him to new and unending life with Christ in God. Lent and Holy Week are preparation for this passover. In the Vigil, we celebrate the Easter sacraments and as a people pass over with Christ from darkness to light, from penitence to rejoicing, from death to life. Throughout the Great Fifty Days, we celebrate Christ's passover and our own. The Vigil ushers in the Great Fifty Days. It begins in Lent and ends in Easter. Easter itself is really both the eighth day of Holy Week, which cannot be planned or celebrated apart from it, and the first day of the Fifty Days we call the Easter season.

The Great Vigil of Easter

The Easter Vigil can be celebrated most effectively with a small group of people, and if your parish has never done it before, you may wish to start small. But if it is planned as a second-class celebration, it will clearly not be seen as the principal liturgy of the year. Many parishes have decided to go "all out" to make the Vigil clearly something special.

What you need are musicians, readers, worshipers, preferably one or more candidates for baptism, and the parish clergy. The Prayer Book says explicitly, "It is customary for all the ordained ministers present, together with lay readers, singers, and other persons, to take active parts in the service" (*BCP*, p. 284). Use not only the clergy but all of the liturgical resources available. Make it self-evidently the work of the worshiping congregation. It does not require great resources, but it does take all that you have.

Set a time between dark and sunrise. Congregations in areas where Easter sunrise services are the rule may wish to begin the Vigil a half hour to an hour before sunrise, ending with the eucharist in the clear light of Easter morning. I can testify from several years of personal experience that this can be very effective. Most places will choose an evening hour, especially if the candidates for baptism are infants. Decide how long you wish the service to last. This will be your primary consideration in choosing the number of readings. There are nine in the Prayer Book. At least two are required. The use of all nine, each followed by a homily, psalm, silence, and collect will produce an "all night" vigil. For a vigil of more moderate length, preach only one homily, after the Gospel, and reduce the number of readings. The reading from Exodus is always used, and a different selection of the others may be used each year. Four to six Old Testament readings are usual.

If at all possible, light the fire outdoors. Beginning the Vigil in a cloister or garden is both appropriate and effective. If there is a parish deacon, the deacon leads the congregation into the dark church carrying the Paschal Candle, the light of Christ scattering the darkness of night. If you have no deacon, then a priest, or the priest, does this. As the procession moves down the aisle, the entire congregation may be given candles lighted from the Easter fire and held during the Exsultet. If they are not needed for the worshipers to see, they may be put out during the readings and relighted for the baptisms. The Exsultet deserves to be sung. If the deacon is not up to it, recruit someone from the choir to sing it, and let the deacon stand beside the book turning the pages.

The lessons may be read by individual lectors, read dramatically by groups, or presented in a number of ways that available talent and imagination may suggest. Use as many different lay people as possible. The psalm or canticle following the reading may be read or sung in any of the ways suggested for the psalm at the eucharist. They need not all be done in the same manner. Some might be sung by the

choir to more difficult or to anthem settings. If there are several priests participating in the Vigil, they share the reading
of the collects among them.

The baptisms may take place either after the final Old Testament reading with its psalm and collect or in the usual
place after the Gospel and sermon. Both choices have their
advantages. If the baptistry is not at the front of the church,
the Paschal Candle is taken from its stand and carried at the
head of the procession to the font. The Prayer for the Candidates (*BCP*, p. 305f) may be sung as a processional litany.
The Thanksgiving over the Water may also be sung. This is
the appropriate occasion on which to sing it. Any priest and
congregation that regularly, or occasionally sings the *sursum
corda* and eucharistic preface can sing the thanksgiving over
the font. After the thanksgiving, the celebrant may sprinkle
the congregation with the baptismal water as a sign of the
renewal of their baptismal vows. The celebration of baptism
was discussed in chapter 6. The Vigil is the most traditional
time for adult baptisms. The preparation of candidates during Lent was discussed in chapter 7. If you are unable to
schedule any baptisms, at least bless the water and sprinkle
the congregation with it after the renewal of vows.

If the font is not at the front of the church, additional
flowers and Easter decorations may be brought into the
sanctuary during the baptism, so that they will be seen
when the procession returns to the altar. Some parishes prefer to vest and decorate the altar during the *Gloria*. Another
possibility is to have the sanctuary decorated for Easter before the beginning of the Vigil but to keep it in darkness, except for the Paschal Candle, until the beginning of the
eucharist and then to turn on the floodlights at the Easter acclamation.

Make the eucharist comparable to your festal Sunday services. Many parishes find it effective to introduce the organ
only at the beginning of the eucharist, using, for example, a
guitar or a recorder to lead the music between the lessons.
The Easter acclamation, "Alleluia. Christ is risen," followed
by the singing of *Gloria in excelsis*, is the occasion for the
pealing of the church bells, the sounding of the organ, and
the breaking forth of Easter joy. Handbells, tambourines, and
every conceivable instrument have been used to enhance

the sense of entry into joy. The acclamation may be said from the baptistry, the procession returning to the sanctuary during the *Gloria.*

If the repeated alleluias and Psalm 114 are not sung between the epistle and Gospel, then an Easter hymn making ample use of "Alleluia" should be sung in its place. Have a Gospel procession, so that the Easter Gospel is seen and heard to be the climax of the many readings from Scripture. At least one parish uses a trumpet before the announcement of the Gospel to make this point. The sermon need not be long, but it must proclaim the good news of the resurrection. If there are adult baptisms, the newly baptized bring up the elements at the offertory. If there are infant baptisms, godparents of the newly baptized do so.

It is important to include familiar Easter hymns in the eucharist. At the offertory, during communion, after communion, and before the dismissal are obvious places. There are many places during the Vigil for the choir to "show its stuff," and singing a cóngregational hymn at the offertory instead of a choir anthem might reduce the strain on both choir and congregation. The service may conclude with the Easter seasonal blessing from *The Book of Occasional Services* (p. 24) and the dismissal with "Alleluia, alleluia" added to it and the response.

A single priest, a song leader, two of three readers, and an enthusiastic congregation, no matter how small, can celebrate the Vigil with great effectiveness. It is better to plan something that you can do well than to try to do too much. But if you plan a celebration suitable for a congregation of fifty in a parish of five hundred communicants, people cannot be blamed for concluding that this is an optional extra for the pious and not the parish's *real* Easter celebration.

Most parishes will lack the resources to celebrate the Vigil "with all the stops pulled out" and then to attempt to do the same thing again on Easter morning. If this is the case, a policy decision is in order. Which service will get the greater share of our resources? Logically and theologically the Vigil should take precedence, but this may be practically and pastorally impossible, especially if the Great Vigil is not deeply embedded in parish tradition. Canonically, the decision is the rector's, but this is precisely the type of decision a parish worship committee is most useful in helping a priest to make. At the very least, they can share the heat for an unpopular decision, but at best they will be good judges of the parish climate and advocates of *good* liturgical change.

Easter Day

If we have avoided the danger of thinking too small in planning the Vigil, we must be wary of going too far in the opposite direction and making the services of Easter Day seem anticlimactic. There will be parishioners for whom the eucharist on Easter Day is the occasion for an infrequent visit to the church. It is good evangelism to make them feel that something significant is going on in which they could be regular participants. There will also be regular churchgoers in whose background the Vigil has had no place and for whom the service on Easter morning is the significant religious event of the year. The resurrection Gospel is, of course, the core of the Liturgy of the Word. In Year A, the Johannine account may be read in place of Matthew, which is the Gospel for the Vigil. The resurrection of Christ and the meaning of our participation in it is the obvious sermon topic. A reading from Acts replaces the Old Testament lesson both today and throughout the Fifty Days. If you wish to use the alternative Old Testament reading, then read Acts in place of the epistle.

Singing familiar Easter hymns is an important way to involve the congregation. Exactly what those hymns are will, of course, vary from congregation to congregation. The parish worship committee may well be better able to identify them than either the rector or the organist. The service almost always will begin with a processional hymn. Incense, processional torches, banners, flags, or whatever says to that congregation, "This is an important occasion!" should be included. The celebrant may wear a cope if that is part of the parish tradition, and the procession may circle the church. The eucharist begins with the Easter acclamation.

Two excellent alternatives to *Gloria in excelsis* for use on Easter morning are "This is the feast of victory for our God" (hymn 417/418) or the Easter canticle "Christ our Passover" (S 16–20, Rite One; S 46–S 50, Rite Two). Alleluia is traditionally sung before the Gospel during Easter. *The Gradual Psalms* contains music for an alleluia chant to be used in this place, or one of the many Easter hymns using alleluia as a refrain may be sung. One way to bind the season together is to use the same alleluia on all the Sundays of Easter. Have a Gospel procession, as described for the Vigil.

Some large parishes may have adult baptisms at the Vigil and infant baptism on Easter Day. The renewal of baptismal vows from the Vigil takes the place of the Nicene Creed. The *Lutheran Book of Worship* and the Methodist supplementary liturgical resource *From Ashes to Fire* recommend sprinkling the people with water from the baptismal font after they have renewed their vows. This is an appropriate ceremony to remind the congregation of their own baptisms, although it is not mentioned in the Prayer Book. A simple explanation of what the renewal of baptismal vows on Easter is all about as a part of the sermon can give people new insights not only into holy water but into the meaning of Easter and of baptism as well.

Increasingly, parishes have felt that the general confession was inappropriate during the Easter festival and have omitted it throughout the Fifty Days. If the entire congregation had participated in the liturgies of Lent and Holy Week, this would certainly be the proper choice. On the other hand, some congregations have felt it important to include the confession of sin in their Easter services to remind us all—especially those who did not participate in the Holy Week liturgies—that sharing in the Easter joy is not without cost. If the confession is omitted, it is helpful, at least on Easter Day, to use a form of the Prayers of the People that includes a petition for the forgiveness of our sins (such as form 1 or 5).

Any of the fraction anthems containing alleluia are suitable for Easter. "At the Lamb's high feast we sing" (hymn 174) is an Easter eucharistic hymn suitable for use during or immediately following communion, although there are many other good choices.

The Fifty Days

The Great Fifty Days are the period of rejoicing in the Risen Lord between the Easter Vigil and Pentecost. During this season the Paschal Candle is lighted at all services and "Alleluia" is sung on all possible occasions. The church is decorated festively. There is no fasting, and traditionally there was no kneeling (although that custom has fallen into disuse in most places). Traditionally, the liturgical color is white, except for the Day of Pentecost, although something can be said for the Sarum rule of using the "best" regardless of color. The church, like the congregation, should be dressed up.

A fixed feature of the Eastertide lectionary is that a lesson from Acts be included. It may replace either the Old Testament reading or the epistle, but it should not be omitted. Planners, even if they are priests, do not always understand this, and I have attended services in which the lesson from Acts was not included, thereby omitting a distinctive Easter feature.

The parish worship committee may also consider other ways of marking the unity of the Fifty Days. The same fraction anthem, for example, may be sung every Sunday. The congregation can stand for the eucharistic prayer and to receive communion, if they regularly kneel, reviving the directive of the Council of Nicea forbidding kneeling during Eastertide.

Lesser Feasts and Fasts contains collects and readings for the weekdays of the Easter season. The first lessons are all from Acts of the Apostles and the Gospels from John. In addition, a rubric there reminds us, "Since the triumphs of the saints are a continuation and manifestation of the Paschal mystery, the celebration of saints' days is particularly appropriate during this season" (p. 56).

Rogation Days

Monday, Tuesday, and Wednesday before Ascension Day are the traditional Rogation Days, although the Prayer Book recognizes the possibility of celebrating them at another time. Their traditional themes are the planting of crops and prayer for their increase. *The Book of Common Prayer 1979* provides three sets of propers: for fruitful seasons, for commerce and industry, for stewardship of creation. The Rogation Days have no real connection with the Fifty Days. It is simply that spring planting occurs at this time in northern Europe. A procession through the fields of the parish blessing the fields was the original English way of celebrating the Rogation. *The Book of Occasional Services* has directions for a Rogation procession (p. 101ff) that may be held on a weekday, concluding with the eucharist, or on a Sunday afternoon as a separate service. In a rural parish in which the parishioners plant crops, this can be an important observance, but it should be scheduled according to the agricultural not the liturgical calendar.

Ascension Day

Ascension Day never falls earlier than April 30 nor later than June 3. Sunset is therefore late, and the weather mild. It is a much neglected opportunity. It is, as Boone Porter has so aptly pointed out, almost tailor-made for an evening service. It can also be the occasion for a parish supper, which is one way to improve attendance on a weekday evening. In many parts of the country, the climate lends itself to the first outdoor service of the season and a picnic supper.

It is important to plan for Ascension Day as a principal feast. Planning small will almost inevitably produce commensurate results. The Ascension Day hymns—such as "See the Conqueror mounts in triumph" (hymn 215), "Hail the day that sees him rise" (hymn 214), or "Alleluia! sing to Jesus" (hymn 460/461)—are among the most singable and popular of our hymns. People should be given an opportunity to sing them. That means planning a service with music. Often the simple expedient of proposing this well ahead of time to the choir, with the suggestion that the choir be the parish's guests at the supper and have their rehearsal afterward, will transform them into eager allies instead of reluctant participants.

The place to begin the actual planning for the service is, as always, with the lectionary. Liturgical planning for a specific service always begins with the appointed lessons. Then it enlarges its concerns to deciding among the various options provided by the Prayer Book and the specific concerns and requirements of the congregation and the occasion. Ascension Day is a part of the Great Fifty Days of Easter, and whatever seasonal planning has been done is a part of your context for the planning of the Ascension Day eucharist. It is especially important that the reading from Acts be included on Ascension Day, since it is the principal scriptural account of the Ascension. It is also proper to use three readings, since Ascension is a major feast. Presumably the first two would be Acts and Ephesians, although you could use Ezekiel and Acts—but not Ezekiel and Ephesians!

There are two choices for the Gospel reading: Luke 24:29-53 and Mark 16:9-15, 19-20. Since Year B is "The Year of Mark," it might seem appropriate to use Mark 16 in that year. But as most New Testament scholars are happy to tell you, with some vigor, this passage is not really a part of Mark but of the so-called long ending. Luke is a less controversial choice. If you do decide to use Mark 16, consider the problems of preaching on it before you print up the programs.

The custom of extinguishing the Paschal Candle after the Gospel on Ascension Day has been rethought and abandoned in most places. The candle is now allowed to burn during the entire Fifty Days of Easter and is extinguished and removed (frequently to the baptistry where it can be lighted for baptisms and from which it can be brought out for funerals) after the last service on Whitsunday.

Even though you are planning a major service for Ascension Day, it is still a workday evening. Simplicity of music and congregational participation are high priorities. This does not mean that you should leave out marks of festivity in your congregation, whether they be incense and deacons in dalmatics or banners in the procession and academic hoods on the lay readers. But lengthy sermons and extended anthems will probably do better on another occasion.

Many large parishes find Ascension Day an opportunity to get people together who attended different Sunday services. Small congregations can use the occasion to have a joint celebration with a neighboring congregation, especially one that shares a priest with them.

Pentecost

Pentecost is, with Easter and Christmas, one of the three major Christian festivals. It is *not* the beginning of the Pentecost season but the final day of the Fifty Days of Easter. The "Season *after* Pentecost" begins the following day. It is a baptismal feast, and planning should include the celebration of Holy Baptism or, at least, the renewal of baptismal vows by the congregation. One advantage of planning for Pentecost over planning for Christmas and Easter is that the festival has not been commercialized. There is no secular observance to take into account.

A number of practical suggestions for making the Pentecost service special have been offered at various times, including having the service outdoors, making it the beginning of a parish strawberry festival, giving out the church school awards, and having a parish picnic following the service. Depending on climate or parish characteristics, some or all of them may be appropriate.

If the Great Vigil of Easter has been a significant baptismal occasion in the parish, there will probably not be many Pentecost baptisms. The Prayer Book (*BCP*, p. 227) provides for the possibility of a Vigil of Pentecost. This is not a true vigil, passing from fast to feast like the Great Vigil, but a sort of repetition of the rites of the Easter Vigil for a second baptismal occasion. Unless there are adult catechumens to be baptized on Pentecost, it is usually better to baptize infants at the principal Pentecost liturgy. If there are no baptisms, the Renewal of Baptismal Vows (*BCP*, p. 292ff) from the Easter Vigil is substituted for the Nicene Creed. The celebrant may compose an introduction similar to that at the Easter Vigil to explain the connection between baptism and the gift of the Holy Spirit. The first Pentecost collect (*BCP*, p. 227) and the Thanksgiving over the Water (*BCP*, p. 306f) will provide the resources.

As throughout Eastertide, the lesson from Acts is significant, and it should always be included among the readings. Many parishes plan to do something special with the readings, based on the question in the lesson from Acts about hearing in our own language. The Acts passage, or a portion of it, or the Gospel may be read in as many different languages as the congregation can find parishioners who speak them. This can often reveal hidden talents among the parishioners. One effective way of doing this is to have several readers in succession each read in a different language Acts 2:1–6 and then finish the lesson in English (or whatever the primary language of the congregation is) beginning with verse 7 and the question about hearing in our own native tongues.

Obviously, the music must be appropriate to the feast and also to the occasion of actual use. Meditative hymns to the

Holy Spirit (such as "Breathe on me, Breath of God," hymn 508) will not work as processional hymns, while an anthem such as "Hail! God the Holy Ghost" will not be suitable during communion. My own choice for the Pentecost procession is "Hail thee, festival day!" to Vaughan Williams' magnificent tune (hymn 225).

10.
The Seasons after
Epiphany and Pentecost

The seasons after Epiphany and Pentecost appear on liturgical calendars as vast expanses of green, the traditional liturgical color for them, broken only by the occasional holy day. Roman Catholics call them "ordinary time." Their calendar does not consider them to be seasons at all but simply "filler" taking up time until the next liturgically significant event. Although Episcopalians call them Sundays after Epiphany and Sundays after Pentecost, we have not really treated them as seasons in the same sense as the others. It is easier, for example, to displace their propers with those of a saint or other festival than in other seasons. Strictly speaking, only Presentation (February 2), Transfiguration (August 6), All Saints (November 1), and the dedication and patronal festivals of the local church may displace a "green" Sunday. The Prayer Book permits "the Collect, Preface, and one or more of the Lessons" for any major feast falling on a "green" Sunday to be substituted for those of the Sunday (*BCP*, p. 16). In practice, this is frequently done whenever possible.

The readings for Epiphany 6, 7, and 8 are the same as those for Propers 1, 2, and 3. Whether they are used after Epiphany or after Pentecost in any given year will depend on whether Easter is early or late. This not only binds the two seasons together, it reinforces the idea that they have no seasonal integrity.

The principal focus of the Sundays is the Lord's Day itself, the weekly commemoration of the resurrection. One of the three prefaces of the Lord's Day is used at the eucharist. There is no proper preface for weekdays after Pentecost, while that of Epiphany may be used in the post-Epiphany season for both weekdays and Sundays.

The Season after Epiphany

This season has a sort of unity and theme, in the series of epiphanies found in the Gospels for the first few Sundays: the baptism, the wedding at Cana (Year C), the healing miracles (Year B), and the transfiguration on the final Sunday after Epiphany. The idea of a seasonal theme, so well expressed in Christopher Wordsworth's great hymn "Songs of thankfulness and praise" (hymn 135), which has been given a new fourth stanza in *The Hymnal 1982* to celebrate the transfiguration, becomes increasingly difficult to sustain when the season is long.

The baptism and transfiguration form a sort of frame for it. They are both festivals of our Lord and may be kept as feasts with white vestments. The Epiphany preface is appointed for both. The Sundays in between are "green" and use either the Lord's Day preface or that of Epiphany. These are the Sundays on which your generically planned Sunday eucharist will require little or no change. They should, nevertheless, be planned as a unit, assuring continuity of sermon themes, ceremonial and musical treatment.

The Post-Pentecost Season

Whatever the season of the Church Year, we, in fact, live in the time between Pentecost and the Parousia. Whether in the cosmic calendar we are at Pentecost 2 or in the week before Advent is not evident. Planning for the post-Pentecost season, then, is planning for *now*. The season itself, to the extent that it can be called a season, begins on the Monday after Pentecost and continues until the Saturday before Advent 1. It is framed by the celebration of Trinity Sunday on the First and Christ the King on the Last Sunday after Pentecost, marked by numbered propers for the Sundays and a number of major and minor holy days on the weekdays. It does not have a seasonal unity other than the consecutive reading of the Gospel: Matthew in Year A; Mark with portions of John 6 on the Sundays in August, following the Markan account of the feeding of the five thousand, in Year B; and Luke, with its wealth of parables, in Year C.

Most places will lack both the interest and the resources for planning extensively for the individual Sundays of the summer. Trinity Sunday often marks the end of the "regular schedule," and unless it is the awarding of church school pins on the following Sunday, nothing much is planned until school reopens in the fall. This is not unreasonable, but some general plans need to be made, which can be applied to the entire sweep of summer Sunday services. Will the services be conducted in the church? If they are, will it be too hot for anyone to worship? Unless your parish borders the Arctic Circle or is air conditioned, the answer to the second question may well be yes, and serious thought needs to be given to dealing with the heat. Otherwise, parishioners will deal with it by staying home.

Summer as a Liturgical Opportunity

Summer can be a time of liturgical opportunity, rather than a low point in the year. It can be used as a time to explore other liturgical formats or other liturgical spaces. Many parishes use the summer for outdoor worship. Planning worship for the open air raises a number of questions beyond the choice of readings.

Most obviously, an alternative plan in case of rain needs to be in place and well known to those who might attend. Wind, insects, and birds need to be considered in choosing places and equipment. Probably some amplification system will be needed if the voices are to be heard outside. Unless prayer books and hymnals are to be taken out for each service, some decisions about common forms that can be printed on a leaflet is essential. An alternative source of music is necessary. It may be a guitar, a person with a strong true voice who will lead the singing, a field organ, or a band. I have heard all used. Will traditional music or folk music be used? This decision will influence and be influenced by the available musicians. Finally, outdoor services need to be kept relatively short, unless there are adequate comfortable seats for a longer service. Many people will wish the service to be short anyway.

Don't simply have the service outdoors. Creatively use the space you have. Pray for the beauty of nature, for rain and sunshine and light and life and health. Many of the Gospel pericopes have settings in fields or at lakes and speak of farming and similar activities. These can be used in the planning.

If the services are to be in the church, it can be decorated with garden flowers. Use simple settings of the service music that the congregation knows. The services can be *planned*, rather than rushed through. Ideally, people should feel they have missed something worthwhile if they are absent; at least they should not be sorry they came. We are talking about at least one-quarter of the Sundays of the year. They are too important to be ignored in your parish's plans for worship.

Planning for Fall

With the reopening of school, the actual planning year of most parishes begins. Like planning for other parish programs, liturgical planning for the fall must be done over the summer so that it is in place by Labor Day. If you wish to make changes in the schedule of services, the opening of school is a convenient time to do so. A reasonable planning procedure would be to plan September and October as a unit, seeking ways to bind the celebrations together so that they do not become unconnected and unending stretches of "green." The use of the lectionary in planning; and setting of seasonal themes for decoration of the church (such as fall flowers); a uniform treatment of the psalm between the readings (singing or reciting it responsorially as described on p. 582 of the Prayer Book, for example); and the use of an appropriate canticle (such as 9, "The First Song of Isaiah," or 19, "The Song of the Redeemed") throughout the period in place of the *Gloria in excelsis* are possible ways to draw the season together.

The month of November, from All Saints to Christ the King, with the building Advent theme, can be a second unit, for which different choices are made. This was discussed in chapter 4 in connection with planning for Advent itself.

Planning for Weekdays

We have been speaking about the planning of Sunday services. Most parishes also have one or more midweek celebrations of the eucharist. Often no thought is given to them in the planning process, and it shows. Parishes with well-planned and celebrated Sunday services often celebrate weekday services in side chapels with the celebrant facing the wall and no thought given to congregational participation. Individual weekday services usually require little planning, other than preparation by the celebrant, but the general framework of such services does need to be planned.

Usually these weekday services are without music, but that does not mean that the celebrant must read everything. Laypersons can (and should) be asked to read the lessons, lead the prayers of the people, and bring the gifts to the altar at the offertory. If another priest or deacon is present at the service, he or she can come forward from the congregation to read the Gospel and to administer the chalice. If a lay eucharistic minister is present, he or she may assist.

If the altar is attached to the wall, its use can be minimized. The entire ministry of the Word may be said from a chair facing the people, and the celebrant may return to the chair for the postcommunion prayer. The important thing to remember about these services is that they are small-group liturgies, not poorly attended Sunday services. Full advantage can be taken of the opportunities for closeness and congregational participation that small groups provide. Their style can be more informal. People may be asked to stand around the altar. Members of the congregation may be encouraged to speak their own prayers aloud at the Prayers of the People.

What difference in the service will there be if a major holy day is being celebrated? Will all of the minor holy days be kept if they occur on the day of the service, or will significant lesser feasts be moved to the days on which there are services? Are there things we can and want to do on weekdays that we can't do on Sundays? Perhaps the clergy and those people who regularly attend these services can be constituted a subcommittee to meet annually to think about these things. It is not an onerous task, but its neglect is often apparent in the ordinary weekday celebrations of many parishes.

11.
Holy Days and Special Occasions

Most holy days fall on weekdays. A few, like Ascension Day and Thanksgiving, always fall on weekdays. But most occur on fixed dates, which generally turn out to be weekdays. Even when the dates fall on Sunday, the prayer book calendar requires the feasts themselves to be transferred to a convenient weekday, at least during Advent, Lent, and Easter. Although strictly speaking only All Saints' Day (November 1), Christmas Day (December 25), Holy Name (January 1), Epiphany (January 6), Presentation (February 2), and Transfiguration (August 6) can be celebrated on Sunday, the Prayer Book permits "the Collect, Preface, and one or more of the Lessons appointed for the Feast [to] be substituted for those of the Sunday, but not from the Last Sunday after Pentecost through the First Sunday after the Epiphany, or from the Last Sunday after the Epiphany through Trinity Sunday" (*BCP*, p. 16)—that is, only on the "green" Sundays. This still permits a good deal of latitude.

The observance of holy days on weekdays usually involves little more than the scheduling of a celebration of the eucharist for the day. Frequently, the feast can be transferred to a day that already has a scheduled weekday service (*BCP*, p. 17). Sometimes an additional eucharist can be scheduled. In an area with more than one Episcopal church it might be possible to schedule a joint celebration for a convenient hour, probably in the evening, which would make a more festive service with music possible. The object is not to have as splendid a service as possible but to enable as many people as possible to join in the celebration and to plan it in such a way that they can see some reason for doing so.

Christmas is clearly a special case and has already been

considered in chapter 5, along with Holy Name and Epiphany. Ascension Day was discussed in chapter 9.

Lesser Feasts

The feasts we have been discussing are major feasts, or "red letter days," so called because they were traditionally printed in red ink by calendar makers, as Sundays and national holidays still are by contemporary printers. The observance of minor feasts, or "black letter days" is purely optional. These days are printed in ordinary type in the prayer book calendar and may be observed using collects and readings from the Common of Saints or propers from *Lesser Feasts and Fasts*. Lesser feasts are never observed on Sunday, unless they are the patronal festival of the congregation. Some congregations will wish to observe all of the lesser feasts and will transfer them, if necessary, to convenient weekdays when services are scheduled. Most congregations will wish to observe some of them. Their observance seldom involves more than using the propers for a weekday eucharist, although St. Francis' Day (October 4) may produce a blessing of pets on the closest Sunday.

Candlemas

Candlemas is the popular name for the Presentation of Our Lord Jesus Christ in the Temple, also called the Purification of St. Mary the Virgin. The name derives from the custom of blessing candles on that day and carrying them in procession. This, in turn, is based on the line from the Song of Simeon that is a part of the Gospel for the day: "A Light to enlighten the nations." The Candlemas Procession finds a place in *The Book of Occasional Services* (p. 51ff). The music is in the Appendix to the Accompaniment Edition of *The Hymnal 1982* (S 340-S 343). It works well before an evening eucharist. It does require enough people to process and to sing, so advance planning and publicity are needed. The procession is completely optional. Some congregations may simply not wish to do it; others may not consider it practical for a weekday evening. Since Presentation is one of the feasts that displaces the Sunday propers when it falls on that day, parishes that do not schedule the procession for a weekday evening may wish to hold one before the parish eucharist in those years in which February 2 is a Sunday.

Candlemas is best begun outside the church with the distribution of candles. The congregation then enters the church in procession carrying the lighted candles. Since Candlemas falls in the dead of winter, in most climates the route of the procession will have to be entirely indoors. It may therefore be necessary to have the procession entirely within the church. A responsorial version of the Song of Simeon, with the refrain "A light to enlighten the nations, and the glory of your people Israel" (S 341), is sung while the candles are being lighted, and appropriate hymns accompany the procession. The procession makes a station, or stop, at some convenient point, and a collect is sung or said. This station may be at the back of the nave if the procession has come in from outside the church or at the chancel step or some other convenient place, such as the baptistry, if the procession has been within the church. Ps. 48:1-2, 10-13 may be sung (S 343) as the procession approaches the altar. The service continues with the *Gloria in excelsis* and the collect of the day.

Michaelmas

St. Michael and All Angels, or Michaelmas, on September 29, is the traditional beginning of the fall or Michaelmas term in England. It has a number of good hymns and may be seized upon as an occasion to plan something special for early fall. Some parishes will choose to bend the prayer book rubrics and celebrate Michaelmas on the last Sunday in September to begin things "in style" in the fall. Others will be content to use the collect at the Prayers of the People and sing one or two of the hymns. Most places will simply observe it on the weekday, celebrating or commemorating it at the Sunday eucharist only if September 29 actually is a Sunday.

All Saints' Day

All Saints' Day calls for a major parish celebration. It may be observed on the Sunday following *in addition to* its observance on the fixed date. While most parishes will wish to make their major observance on Sunday, the possibility of an evening service on November 1, with the opportunity to sing more of the All Saints' Day hymns, should not be overlooked. A parish dinner and evening program might make for a significant evening of prayer and good fellowship in the congregation. The lectionary gives alternative sets of readings. One set may be chosen for the feast day eucharist and the other used the following Sunday.

All Saints' Day is one of the baptismal feasts, and an effort should be made to schedule baptisms for the Sunday eucharist (or the weekday service if that works better in your congregation). Notices in parish newsletters in the late summer and at the start of church school should mention the time and date, urging those with children to be baptized to come forward. Occasions for the preparation of parents and godparents should be included in the fall schedule. If this custom is maintained year after year, people will begin to think in terms of All Saints' Day as a day for baptisms and to plan to invite family and friends for the occasion.

At those celebrations at which there are no baptisms, the Renewal of Baptismal Vows from the Easter Vigil (*BCP*, p. 292) can be included. A simple introduction explaining the baptismal significance of All Saints' Day and the relationship of baptism to our membership in the Church and the communion of saints would be appropriate.

I have had little experience with the interesting All Hallows' Eve vigil in *The Book of Occasional Services* (p. 106ff). But someone with imagination can do something attractive to young people by including that material.

All Souls' Day

The commemoration of All Faithful Departed, often called All Souls' Day, is November 2. The late John Heus, former rector of St. Matthew's, Evanston, and Trinity, New York, described All Souls' Day as the feast of the Christian democracy. All Saints' Day honors the heroes of the Church throughout the ages, while All Souls' Day remembers *all* of our fellow Christians who have gone before us. I have found the distinction most useful and free from overtones of "purgatory." The Sunday celebration will almost necessarily include some recognition of all the faithful departed in the eucharist, and this should be well thought out in the planning.

Thanksgiving Day

Thanksgiving Day is an American national holiday that is appropriately observed by a service of thanksgiving in church. The eucharist is the traditional Christian service of thanksgiving. *The Book of Common Prayer* includes Thanksgiving in the list of major feasts and includes propers for the eucharist and the daily offices.

Since it will always occur in the two weeks before the First Sunday in Advent, it can be a regular part of your seasonal planning. The theme of thanksgiving can be blended with the seasonal themes, remembering that we give thanks "above all for [God's] immeasurable love in the redemption of the world by our Lord Jesus Christ" (*BCP*, p. 125). A Litany of Thanksgiving (*BCP*, p. 836f) may be used in place of the Prayers of the People at the eucharist. Decoration of the church with harvest fruits and fall flowers and the singing of familiar Thanksgiving Day hymns are important to most worshipers and should figure in the planning. Using home-baked bread and local wine, even if you do not usually do so, can help people make the connection between the Lord's Table and the Thanksgiving dinner table.

The Patronal and Dedication Festivals

The prayer book calendar mentions "the feast of the Dedication of a Church, and the feast of its patron or title" as feasts that "may be observed on, or be transferred to, a Sunday, except in the seasons of Advent, Lent, and Easter" (*BCP*, p. 16). The feast of title is the festival that gives its name to the church building. If the title is a saint's name, the saint is called the patron of the church, and its festival is the patronal festival. The feast of the dedication is the anniversary of the consecration of a church. Every consecrated church can have both. Almost inevitably one will come at an inconvenient time, and most congregations pick one festival a year to celebrate as their parish festival. In 1536, the English convocations directed that churches that did not know when their dedication festival was should keep it on the first Sunday in October, and this is commonly done in England. The idea of picking a convenient Sunday for a parish festival has much to commend it, particularly if the actual dates make celebration difficult.

If it can be kept on a Sunday, most churches will prefer to do so. But a glorious celebration can be held on a weekday evening, including a parish supper and entertainment. There are no special ceremonies for the liturgy, except that it should be done as on the principal festivals. Prayers for the parish and congregation, and for those who founded and maintained it, should be included in the Prayers of the People. A Litany of Thanksgiving for a Church (*BCP*, p. 578f) may be used in place of the usual forms. If this is to be a true festival, the liturgy should be the centerpiece of a larger celebration involving as much of the congregation as possible. Perhaps a brunch, a picnic, a party, or whatever suggests itself to the people of the parish can be planned to follow the eucharist. Like an individual's birthday party, the patronal and dedication festivals of a parish are their own special feasts.

The Bishop's Visitation

The bishop's visitation is not simply the occasion for a confirmation service; it is an important event in the cycle of the liturgical year. Frequently, this is insufficiently appreciated by both bishops and parishes. The scheduling of the visitation is largely in the hands of the bishop's office, and parishes are presented with times and schedules that are part of the "given" for their own planning. The visitation will undoubtedly include a reception for the congregation and may include meetings with clergy and vestry.

The Prayer Book's liturgical expectations are that the bishop will preach the Word of God, preside at the eucharist and baptism, and administer confirmation. It is especially appropriate for the bishop to baptize adults, and if there are adult candidates, the bishop should be notified as soon as possible. The bishop may also baptize infants, and some bishops are anxious to do so. Most will do so if they understand that the parish (not just the rector) is serious about wanting them to do so. If adults have been baptized or received by the parish priest at the Easter Vigil or one of the other baptismal feasts, they should be presented to the bishop at this time to have that action confirmed, which is probably the original meaning of the term in this context. Candidates for confirmation are "to make a mature public affirmation of their faith and commitment to the responsibilities of their Baptism" (*BCP*, p. 412). This would imply that they were not children.

The service, whether on a weekday evening or a Sunday, should be planned for the entire congregation, not just the families of the confirmands. If the service is on Sunday afternoon or evening, the morning schedule should be altered to make the bishop's eucharist clearly the chief service of the day. The bishop is the chief celebrant. The priests of the parish may stand at the altar with the bishop as a sign of their shared pastoral responsibility for the congregation. The deacon, if there is one, should be at the bishop's right, both at the chair and at the altar. The deacon or an acolyte holds the pastoral staff, when the bishop is not carrying it. The other liturgical ministers of the parish should fill their customary roles: lectors, ushers, ministers of communion.

If the service is on a Sunday or holy day, the propers are normally those of the day. On other days, the propers "At Baptism" (or if there is no baptism, "At Confirmation") are used, and the bishop may designate one or more of those lessons to be used on any day. If there are baptisms, the service is conducted as described in chapter 6. The parts of the service marked in the Prayer Book by a solid line are added for confirmation. The bishop may consecrate chrism after the thanksgiving over the water or bring chrism from the cathedral. If the bishop will consecrate chrism, the oil needs to be prepared beforehand—olive oil and some aromatic substance traditionally called balsam. A good pharmacist can help you find something suitable, or "chrism essence" can be bought from a church supply house. They are mixed either before the service or immediately before the bishop says the prayer. The chrism is left in the parish for use by the priest at baptisms during the coming year.

The bishop may ask the parish priest to pour the water over the candidates, but the bishop personally signs the newly baptized. This may be done from the chair at the front of the nave or the center of the chancel where the bishop has presided over the presentation and examination of the candidates. After the welcoming of the newly baptized, the bishop lays hands on the candidates for confirmation, reception, and reaffirmation. The peace follows (*BCP*, p. 309f).

If there are no baptisms, the Confirmation service (*BCP*, pp. 413-419) is used, with appropriate propers. The bishop's chair is placed in the center of the choir or at the front of the nave. The entire congregation renews its baptismal vows with the candidates. The bishop may consecrate the chrism for the parish, even if there are no baptisms. In that case, it is done immediately after the postcommunion prayer according to the form in *The Book of Occasional Services* (p. 224f).

The bishop visits the parish as its chief pastor and priest. Care should be taken in planning to see that it does not resemble a royal visit. The planning committee also needs to consider the probable length of the service. Longer and impressive are not synonyms. If there are many things happening, many candidates for baptism, confirmation, and reception, the service will be long, but it need not be needlessly lengthened by including additional hymns, solos, or choral anthems. On the other hand, the music should represent the parish at its best.

Liturgical Books
Mentioned in the Text

The Book of Common Prayer refers to the edition authorized by the General Convention of the Episcopal Church in 1979. It is the official liturgy of the Episcopal Church (USA). It is not copyrighted and is published by several publishers in various editions. Page numbers are identical in all editions.

The Altar Book is an excerpt from the Book of Common Prayer arranged for the convenience of the chief celebrant at the eucharist. It contains musical notation for most parts of the service which may be sung by the priest. It is published by Church Hymnal Corporation.

Lesser Feasts and Fasts (Fourth Edition) is an official publication of the Episcopal Church, authorized by General Convention. It contains the collects and lectionary references for minor holy days and the weekdays of Lent and Eastertide, as well as brief biographies of the saints. The present edition was authorized in 1988. The book is copyrighted by the Church Pension Fund, but congregations may reproduce portions for their own use without charge or written permission.

The Book of Occasional Services contains services for occasions not in the Book of Common Prayer. The second edition was authorized by the General Convention of 1988. It is also copyrighted by the Church Pension Fund, but congregations may reproduce portions for their own use without charge or written permission.

The Hymnal 1982 actually appeared in 1985. It is the official hymnal of the Episcopal Church. Volume One of the Accompaniment Edition includes an appendix containing music not in the pew edition, much of it with permission to reproduce. It also includes a section entitled "Resources for Service Planning" containing a number of indices.

Gradual Psalms is a four–volume publication of the Standing Commission on Church Music available from Church Hymnal Corporation. They contain plainsong settings of the psalms to be sung between the readings at the eucharist, with appropriate refrains, and texts for Alleluia verses to be sung before the Gospel. Congregations may reproduce the individual pages for their own use without charge or written permission.

The Book of Alternative Services of the Anglican Church of Canada was authorized by the General Synod of that church in 1983 as an alternative to the Canadian Prayer Book. It is published by Anglican Book Centre, Toronto.

For Further Reading

Associated Parishes. *Celebrating Redemption: The Liturgies of Lent, Holy Week, and the Great Fifty Days.* Alexandria, Va.: Associated Parishes, 1980.

――――. *The Great Vigil of Easter: A Commentary.* Alexandria, Va.: Associated Parishes, 1977.

――――. *Holy Eucharist, Rite Two: A Commentary.* Alexandria, Va.: Associated Parishes, 1976.

――――. *Parish Eucharist.* Alexandria, Va.: Associated Parishes, 1977.

――――. *The Parish Worship Committee.* Alexandria, Va.: Associated Parishes, 1988.

Cassa, Yvonne, and Sanders, Joanne. *Groundwork: Planning Liturgical Seasons.* Chicago: Liturgy Training Publications, 1982.

Crichton, J. D. *Christian Celebration.* London: Geoffrey Chapman, 1973.

Eastman, A. Theodore. *The Baptizing Community.* Harrisburg: Morehouse, 1991.

Galley, Howard. *The Ceremonies of the Eucharist.* Cambridge: Cowley, 1989.

Glover, Raymond, ed. *The Hymnal (1982) Companion.* New York: Church Hymnal, 1991.

Guilbert, Charles M. *Words of Our Worship.* New York: Church Hymnal, 1989.

Hatchett, Marion J. *Commentary on the Book of Common Prayer.* New York: Seabury, 1980.

――――. *A Guide to the Practice of Church Music.* New York: Church Hymnal, 1989.

――――. *Hymnal Studies Five: A Liturgical Index to the Hymnal 1982.* New York: Church Hymnal, 1985.

Michno, Dennis. *A Priest's Handbook.* 2d ed. Wilton: Morehouse-Barlow, 1986.

Middleton, A. Pierce. *Old Wine in New Skins.* Wilton: Morehouse-Barlow, 1988.

Mitchell, Leonel L. *Praying Shapes Believing: A Theological Commentary on the Book of Common Prayer.* Harrisburg: Morehouse, 1991.

————. *The Way We Pray: An Introduction to the Book of Common Prayer.* Cincinnati: Forward Movement, 1984.

New Westminster Dictionary of Liturgy and Worship. Philadelphia: Westminster, 1986.

Pregnall, William S. *Laity and Liturgy: A Handbook for Parish Worship.* New York: Seabury, 1975.

Porter, H. Boone. *The Day of Light: The Biblical and Liturgical Meaning of Sunday.* New York: Seabury, 1960. Reprint. Washington: Pastoral Press, 1987.

————. *Keeping the Church Year,* New York: Seabury, 1977.

Price, Charles, and Weil, Louis. *Liturgy for Living.* Church's Teaching Series. New York: Seabury, 1979.

Price, Charles. *Introducing the Book of Common Prayer.* New York: Church Hymnal, 1988.

Ramshaw, Gail, ed., *Intercessions for the Christian People.* New York: Pueblo, 1988.

Sansom, Michael. *A Liturgical Glossary.* Grove Liturgical Study 42. Bramcote, Notts, England: Grove Books, 1985.

Schmemann, Alexander. *For the Life of the World: Sacraments and Orthodoxy.* Crestwood, New York: St. Vladimir's Seminary Press, 1973.

Standing Liturgical Commission. *Commentary on Prayer Book Studies 30: Supplementary Liturgical Texts.* New York: Church Hymnal, 1989.

Stevenson, Kenneth. *Jerusalem Revisited: The Liturgical Meaning of Holy Week.* Washington: Pastoral Press, 1988.

Stuhlman, Byron D. *Prayer Book Rubrics Expanded.* New York: Church Hymnal, 1987.

Webber, Christopher, L. *A New Metrical Psalter.* New York: Church Hymnal, 1986.